You C[...]
Attract It

Steve G. Jones, Clinical Hypnotherapist
Frank Mangano, Health Advocate

Strategic Book Publishing
New York, NewYork

Strategic Book Publishing
An imprint of Strategic Book Group
P.O. Box 333
Durham CT 06422
www.StrategicBookGroup.com

ISBN: 978-1-60860-759-4

Printed in the United States of America

We have created a blog especially for you! We want to encourage you to check it out:
http://www.YouCanAttractIt.com/blog.
We both contribute fun and informative articles several times a week. The blog is all about the Law of Attraction. We give you extra tools and tips to help you incorporate the Law of Attraction into your life…and it's all for free!

Contents

Foreword

Several months ago, I was invited to review this book and hesitated due to not personally knowing the authors and thinking that I have read just about everything there is to read about the Law of Attraction.

I also thought I knew everything there was to know about it—a little presumptuous due to the personal success I have had in transforming my own life using many of the principles and techniques in this book.

After reading it, however, I realized that Frank and Steve had a wonderful way of not just explaining the Law of Attraction so that anyone could really grasp it, but they also show the reader how to make the necessary changes from the inside out so that the Law of Attraction works day and night.

Many people think that having positive thoughts, wishing, praying, meditating and hoping all day long is the key to *attracting* what you desire in your life. It's not. If you do just that, you will be in for a very shocking reality. It doesn't work.

This book will show you that there are very specific language patterns that you must use to retrain your brain so that your conscious and subconscious thoughts line up with whatever you want to manifest in your life.

In addition to *being* in the right vibration, you must also adopt the right beliefs to match the desired outcome in each area of your life. This book will show you step by step how to transform negative, destructive thoughts, feelings, and actions to positive, constructive thoughts, feelings, and actions that match your goals and dreams in each area of your life.

Is it better health you want? More money? To stop smoking? A better relationship? Each of us has hopes and dreams of living a wonderful life, yet we each have negative neurological patterns that stop us from reaching our true potential.

What I love about this book is that Frank and Steve break down the different areas of life into easy-to-follow sections that you can just choose, learn, and apply.

This book is not one you just read and put down. You interact with it and refer to it over and over again. It's more of a do-it-yourself guide that will help you reshape and improve any area of your life. Many people have heard of hypnosis but do not really understand how this powerful tool can help them transform any negative habit they have.

First and foremost, all hypnosis is self–hypnosis, and a hypnotist cannot get you or anyone else to do what you do not want to do. That is a fallacy that has been propagated by the shows we see in Las Vegas or on television.

Learning how to induce a *self-hypnotic* state is brilliantly explained in this book so that anyone can master his own lasting change from the inside out.

I highly recommend that you read this book and apply what you learn immediately. I know without a shadow of a doubt that what is contained within these pages can and will transform your life forever.

I wish you all the success that you desire.

John Assaraf
New York Times best-selling author

Acknowledgments

First and foremost, we could not have written this book without each other's help, experience, and insight on the Law of Attraction. Without each other, this book would not have been possible. We are both thankful for the support of Frank's mother and father, Patricia and Frank, who provided us with continuous and unwavering support and encouragement throughout this project. We want to give a very special thanks to Katherine Sinclair for assisting us in our research. We want to thank one of the experts featured in the film and book *The Secret,* John Assaraf, for his invaluable input. Also a very special thanks to Nicole Maresca, who provided editorial assistance; to Paul Mascetta for his support during this book project, and to all of our loyal readers for their continued support. We thank the universe for allowing this to come to fruition as it has. Last, but certainly not least, we are grateful to God for giving us this opportunity to help others.

Introduction

The Law of Attraction (LOA) is far from a new concept. Stemming from Hinduism, this spiritual and esoteric theory has evolved greatly since ancient times. The reason we have decided to write a book about the many teachings and different theories of the LOA is quite simply due to our own positive personal experiences, which we hope to share with you. The principles of the LOA can and should be used in your everyday life, but without taking the proper steps and educational avenues, you may not be using the LOA effectively.

You may be wondering just how it is possible to literally change how your mind works and how you think. We are going to show you that this is within your control and how to use these theories to their full potential in your own life. You do not have to be a spiritual teacher to make the LOA work for you, but you do have to possess a great deal of discipline and confidence in the LOA to make it work.

Throughout this book we will reveal to you the secrets of these concepts that we have used to further advance our professional and personal lives. You too can take the concepts and theories of the LOA and change your life in a positive way that you never thought could even be possible. There is no need to feel stress and anxiety on a day-to-day basis and live a life that was nothing like what you've always dreamed of. The LOA can help you take control of your life and change certain areas, allowing you to create an entirely new view of life itself.

In this book, we will provide you with the definitions of concepts as they apply to the LOA. We will explain the six steps of the LOA, with exercises and suggestions for applying them in your own life. You will notice that the chapters containing the six steps are interspersed with chapters on other topics. This has been done deliberately in order to make you, the reader, aware of various concepts along the way and show the many facets of life to which the LOA can be applied.

This book will take you through each and every step of the LOA process to help you learn how to use it. It will also make sure that you understand each and every principle thoroughly. When you have finished reading this book, you will be able to transform any part of your life by putting these principles into action!

We suggest reading this book in one of two ways. You can read it all the way through, then go back and study the steps, focusing on each one until you have mastered it. Or, you can take your time in familiarizing yourself with and incorporating each step into your life before reading the next step. You will have to do what works best for you. Whichever method you choose, we want to make it clear that you must do all the work you need to do with each step before moving on to the next one. As you read, you will realize the importance of each step and the potential impact it can have on your life. These steps are meant to be read with an open mind. We wish you great success!

Let's get started! Please read through each and every word carefully to make sure you are not missing even one little thing, as that can make the difference between your own personal success and failures. Do not become discouraged if you do not see immediate results with the LOA as it takes time. Trust us, your patience will be worth it!

1

Personal Stories

To get started, we thought it would be beneficial to share our personal life stories and how the LOA has changed certain aspects of our lives and created an entirely new mindset to our approach to life. We hope you are as excited as we are to begin this journey. The LOA can open many new doors for those who use its principles correctly.

STEVE'S STORY

I want to share my story about how using the LOA has helped me in my financial, personal, physical, and spiritual successes. First of all, the LOA is based on believing that you are going to get what you hope for. Beyond believing in the LOA intellectually, you must also be able to go deeper, and emotionally feel good things coming to you. You need an emotional reason for whatever you want to bring into your life.

For me, financially speaking, that part was easy. I had been practicing hypnotherapy since the mid-1980s, and I had enjoyed a tremendous amount of financial success. However, I was not building wealth because my money was going toward extravagant rent for my Beverly Hills office and my home in Marina del Rey, both of which I was renting. All of the money I was making was going right through my hands; I was allowing this to happen. I became very frustrated with my financial situation. I started envisioning a future in which I would own property, build wealth, and have investments.

For me the main trick in becoming financially successful was letting go of my ego. I had to separate myself from my attachment to my Beverly Hills office. I realized that equating my office location with success was only serving my ego. I felt that others perceived the location of my office as a status symbol, and indeed it was, but at the same time it was emotionally, physically, and financially draining me. The drive to and from my office every day was also draining me physically. I was always stuck in traffic, and it took me at least an hour to get to and from work. The long hours were also physically draining. On top of seeing patients, I was running an online hypnotherapy business that took a lot out of me physically and emotionally.

I simply envisioned a new place to live, and I then began to change my life. What came to mind for me was a place I had visited: Savannah, Georgia. Anyone who has been to Savannah knows that it has a lot of charm. All the streets are lined with oak trees, and everything moves a little slower in Savannah compared to Los Angeles. I made the decision that I would move there.

The process was almost like throwing a dart on a map because although this was the place that immediately came to mind, I didn't really know much about living and working in Savannah. I didn't know anyone in the town. I didn't own a house yet and I didn't have a Lexus, but in my mind I could see the house and the car. I could imagine a better life where I looked forward to growing my business. I knew I could reach my goals because I could envision my new life. I painted a very detailed picture of all of this in my mind.

Financially, moving to Savannah made sense. Home prices were reasonable and office space would be easy to find. I envisioned buying a house so my monthly payments went toward ownership rather than rent. I wanted to get into real estate investing by owning rental property. I envisioned living a stress-free life. I envisioned having investments. I envisioned driving a Lexus. I envisioned having my physical vitality back and loving my low-stress life. I made sure that I knew exactly what I wanted. It was only when I knew exactly what I wanted that I was able to go after it.

Of course, when I moved to Savannah, I didn't have enough money to buy a house or a car. At first I rented an apartment; since the cost of living is a lot lower in Savannah, I was able to save for a down payment on a house. I put a lot of focus and attention into my hypnotherapy practice and website. In less than a year, my website sales had doubled, and I was able to put a down payment on my first house. Now, instead of my money going toward rent, it was going toward a mortgage and home ownership.

Even after one year had passed since I had moved and set my goals, I still woke up every morning envisioning my goals and the life I truly wanted. Every day I looked forward to working with my patients and developing my website because my practice and my business were growing. Every day I was getting closer to realizing my dreams. I owned my house, but I was still envisioning a rental property, investing, and a Lexus parked in my driveway. Although I was still working long hours, I wasn't stressed about it. I didn't feel pressure, I felt motivated! I was enjoying my work, and I no longer had to put up with Los Angeles traffic!

One year later (two years after moving), all of my dreams and visions really started to fall into place. My business doubled its sales. At this point I decided it was important to invest my money instead of letting it sit in the bank. I found a financial adviser who helped me find the right investments for my lifestyle. I also decided that it was time for me to purchase that Lexus I had been envisioning. Now the Lexus was actually in my driveway and I owned it!

A few months later I was looking at various island properties around Savannah. I found a bigger house on an amazing piece of land. The house had ten rooms, two and a half bathrooms, a fireplace, dock, Jacuzzi, two-car garage, and an amazing view of the marsh. I wound up getting a great deal on the house because it needed some work, but I was willing to get my hands a little dirty for the house I had been envisioning. It took a couple of months of manual labor to create my ideal home, but it was well worth the sweat. I quickly moved into my new house and decided not to sell my other house; I turned it into rental property.

I was starting to fully realize the power of the LOA. I no longer had to picture in my mind a marsh-front house or a rental property because now I had them both. I no longer had to envision a Lexus in my mind; I could just go into my garage and see it. I received monthly statements from my investment company showing me how my money was growing. All of this happened for me because I held this vision steady in my mind as I moved forward. Not a day went by when I didn't think about my goals and envision myself achieving them.

It's important to point out again that in using the LOA it is imperative that you have an emotional attachment to the changes you want. I had a strong emotional attachment to what I wanted because I was truly fed up with my lifestyle and I was ready for a change. Here I am three years later having achieved my goals and realized my vision. The house I live in is on an island and I have my own private dock. When I look out of one of the many back windows, I can see dolphins swimming by. My rental property is less than a mile down the road, and it brings in monthly rental income. I know my money is safe in my investments. I am going to leave my money in those investments for a long time so that it will grow, just like I have these past few years. I'm enjoying my Lexus, especially since I'm never sitting in traffic. All of this happened for me simply as a result of recognizing a strong, emotionally based reason for wanting a change, believing in that reason, and attracting the change to myself.

I want to share something amazing with you. Even though I have realized my goals and I am now living my dreams, I am still attracting abundance in my life. This is what is so wonderful about the LOA. Great things keep coming to me. I lead a fulfilling and successful life and the LOA continues to reward me.

Currently, I am focused on expanding my Web site business to include greater product offerings. A year from now I envision myself having doubled my sales yet again. I work long days, but again, I don't feel any stress; I feel motivation. I spend my time seeing patients, teaching students, working on my doctorate degree, and overseeing my online business, for which I have had to hire staff: a Web designer, two full-time sound engineers, and a full-time office manager to keep it all going. By wanting and believing in a stress-free life, I have attracted fantastic employees that make my life and my job a lot easier.

I want you to realize that it could take a little while for you to reach your goals, or it could be practically overnight. The important thing to remember is to keep envisioning your goals; the things you want and need out of your life. Be patient and keep your focus. Since I have attracted my original vision, I have created new ones. Now there are new things that I would like to attract into my life. And I know that in time, the universe will reward me with my visions.

Throughout this book you are going to receive great tips on how you can make the LOA work for you. The goal of this book is to get you to believe in the LOA and teach you to envision changes in your own life. I encourage you to open your mind, body, and soul to the LOA. Right now I am excited for you because you are about to embark on something very powerful and life-changing.

FRANK'S STORY

For me, vision was the most important feature of the LOA and what I found to be most important in my life. I have always had strong visions about how I wanted to live my life. Ever since I was young, I dreaded the idea of working for someone else. In my mind, working for someone else was downright painful. I personally never understood why people put their lives in the hands of others and, in some cases, subjected themselves to abuse in the process.

I knew there had to be another way. I just didn't exactly know how to pave the road I knew I wanted to take when I was younger so I temporarily had to take a few jobs that I disliked very much to make ends meet. After a few years of bouncing around from job to job, I found myself working for a nonprofit charity organization. This particular job was probably as close to what I considered tolerable at the time because I did find a sense of joy and fulfillment in the work. The pay and some of the people I worked for were another story, however, and left much to be desired. I knew this job (once again) was just not for me.

During my employment for the nonprofit, my mother was prescribed medication to lower her cholesterol. Being raised in a household full of vitamins, supplements, and books on home remedies, the family did not take this news well. I immersed myself in research to figure out a natural method that my mother could use to lower her cholesterol without using the medication that was riddled with potential harmful side effects.

After months of research, I finally created what I now call the *Mangano Method* for lowering cholesterol naturally. It worked, and my mother did not have to take cholesterol medication as her doctors had said she would. I decided I wanted to help as many people as possible lower their cholesterol naturally and without harmful side effects, so I decided to write a book about it. What better way to reach a ton of people? I ran into a big problem when I discovered that you could be giving away free gold, but if you've never written a book before or don't have any sort of a following, publishing companies are not exactly lining up to help you (they are now, though; more on that later). As a result, I decided to publish the book myself in electronic format on the Internet. I created a website and sold a few books here and there.

Even though I was not yet making any money from the book, I was gaining something much more rewarding than cash—the sense of accomplishment that comes with knowing that you created something that is helping others and in the process of doing so, you enjoyed every moment. I felt like I was truly beginning to realize my passion. If I could dedicate myself to in-depth research on one medical condition and create an effective method to treat it, why could I not do it with others? It was at that moment that I realized my destiny and the direction I wanted my life to take.

I went to work on my next e-book, which involved the use of the *Mangano Method* once again, only this time it was structured around treating and preventing hypertension, otherwise known as high blood pressure. It was a success. I then realized that as fulfilled as I felt from helping others through these two books, I wanted to reach a wider audience. I wanted to reach people that were dealing with all kinds of ailments. Most of all, I wanted to offer it for free. I looked at it as kind of a hobby that I did to keep myself sane while working my day job. So I created a website that would serve as a free resource for information on treating and preventing many aliments, diseases, sicknesses, viruses and conditions safely, naturally, and without the use of harmful medications. Each week, I set a goal to research a different condition and find a natural method for treating or preventing it. As the site grew, I began making just enough money to pay for the cost of the research through advertising. I knew I wanted to eventually turn my passion and desire to explore natural health and alternative medicine into a business that I could profit from. After all, I did still have bills to pay.

Before I go any further, I want to be clear on one thing that I now know to be unequivocally true: Reality is nothing more than your acceptance of it. If you truly believe that your reality should be a certain way, it will become so. Regardless of whether they are positive or negative, your thoughts ultimately create your reality.

At the time, I did not have an *abundance* mentality. To be honest, I had a *just enough to get by* mentality. And because of that, I just got by—and that was it. To have a true abundance mentality is to believe that you are entitled to all the great things that life has to offer in the form of whatever brings you joy, fulfillment, and happiness. I believed that I was entitled to do what I love, which is to help people, but I was not sold on the fact that I was entitled to make a good living doing so. As a result, my reality was just that—I helped people but didn't make much money in the process.

I then met a woman with whom I fell deeply in love. We dated for a while and eventually things began getting more serious. As we talked about our future together, I started to realize that we had two completely different ideas of what work should be. I had always believed in the entrepreneurial spirit where you work for yourself and call your own shots. Heck, even though I wasn't making much money at what I was doing, to me that was worth more than having to answer to a boss that wants to see a death certificate when you need time off because someone in your family passed away!

She, on the other hand, felt that owning one's own business was too risky. Her mentality was to get a steady nine-to-five job (preferably for a government or city organization), work yourself to the bone in a structured setting, and retire in twenty years. Aside from that, she knew very little about the power of the Internet. The fact that I was thinking of pursuing a business online made her feel as though I was taking an even bigger risk and wasting my time by not getting a real job. I knew deep down she was wrong, but the heart wants what the heart wants. And at that time, my heart wanted nothing more than to be with her. And so, I began taking classes to learn how to drive a school bus and eventually got my CDL license. My friends and family thought I had completely lost my mind. Here I was, never a morning person, a guy who talked his whole life about never working for anyone else, getting up at three thirty every morning to go and take orders from a dispatcher and drive a bus for $400 a week for perhaps the rest of my life!

Influence from another source can affect one's decision-making process dramatically. Couple that with the fact that I had a *just-get-by* mentality, and what you have (and what I was) is a person who is flushing his dreams down the drain and setting himself up for a life of misery because his vision had become distorted.

As you will learn, one of the key elements to achieving success is having a clear vision of what you want. This is especially important when using the LOA because if you cannot clearly visualize what you want, you cannot begin the process of attracting it. Simply put, you cannot attract what you cannot visualize. What is worse is when you visualize things that you do not want because that's what you begin to attract. In essence, the vision that I had for my professional life was being overpowered by the vision that I had for my personal life. The result was that I was beginning to attract things into my life that I really didn't want.

Realizing that my life was headed in the wrong direction, I voiced my feelings to my significant other. However, my words fell on deaf ears, and eventually we went our separate ways. I was devastated and heartbroken for months. I was depressed, sad, lonely, and just plain miserable. But the one thing I wasn't was in conflict anymore.

The vision that I had for my professional life was no longer being distorted, and any negative influence that I had once been receiving from my girlfriend was now gone. And that's when some amazing things began happening for me. My vision for my professional life really started to become crystal clear once I immersed myself in my business. Little by little, opportunities and resources began coming my way, and within a year, I was able to quit my job, achieve complete financial independence, and even land a deal with a publishing company for a book that has become a bestseller on Amazon.com and Barnes & Noble.

Looking back now, I find that a big problem was being surrounded by too much negativity. Perhaps the most important factor in using the LOA is to clear yourself of all negative thoughts and behaviors. It became clear to me that surrounding myself with negativity was not beneficial. Negative people equal negative energy, and no matter what you do, this negative energy eventually rubs off. In order to get rid of this negative influence in my life, I was forced to isolate myself from anyone who was instilling it in me just by being associated with him or her. This actually took years to figure out but was the most important step in my life. As I stated earlier, I had always had this vision, but what I did not have was the road to take to make it happen. Once I cleared myself of negative influences, I found it much easier to eliminate the negative feelings, thoughts, and emotions from within myself as well. It was only at this time in my life that I was able to start my own business and begin helping others, which, to this day, gives me a tremendous sense of accomplishment and joy.

I was finally able to help myself through my new business and state of mind. Today I reside in a beautiful New York City neighborhood, I run a successful publishing company, and I help many people on a daily basis. Once I was able to clearly see my vision and understand what I really wanted, it became easier and easier to make the right choices and decisions that made this all happen. My business became successful and I now have the ability to drive the kind of car I want to drive, and do many other things that I've always wanted. It literally became a dream come true when my business continued to grow to the point where I needed to hire others to help me continue this growth. This, for me, is the dream come true that I live on a daily basis.

All of this was only possible because of the right state of mind that I eventually adopted, combined with the proper use of the LOA.

2

What is the Law of Attraction?

Many people have recently become aware of the LOA due to the major publicity it has been receiving lately. It is a term of which you may have heard but of which you do not know the definition. Additionally, you may not know how to use it for beneficial purposes in your own life. It is the simple concept that what one puts out into the universe is exactly what one gets back. There are many different terms for this. In the 1960s it was called Karma. Right now you may be thinking the basic concept is "you get what you deserve." No matter what you choose to call it, the idea is still the same—what you put out there is what you get in return.

The concept has been a fixture of many religious standards, including the Bible and the Koran. These are concepts that worked successfully in ancient times and still work today. At its core, the LOA states that if you think positive thoughts, you will receive positive experiences and get what you want out of life. If you think negative thoughts, you will receive negative experiences. Let us be clear that we are not speaking of the intellectual thoughts that help you calculate mathematics. We are talking about your conscious and subconscious thoughts, which are on a more emotional level and can have an extreme impact your life.

If you feel anger toward the world, you will receive anger back from it. If you feel nothing but happiness toward the world, that is exactly what you will experience in return. If you feel abundance or wealth toward the world, this is what you will get back. You can see how the LOA can provide you with the life of your dreams with the proper mindset. The LOA encompasses all of your thoughts, feelings, visualizations, and actions. In turn, all four of these aspects directly contribute to the LOA. You must be fully aware of each one and make sure that you are putting positive energy out there for the universe in order to receive positive things in return.

You may be wondering what me mean when we use the word *universe*. The universe is more than just space and a bunch of stars and planets. When we use the term *universe,* we are referring to space, time, matter, and most important, energy and laws. In relation to physics, the universe is defined as everything that exists, has existed, and will exist. The idea that the universe already holds what will exist is where the idea of the LOA is held. Whatever you want to attract into your life with the LOA already exists. You just have to learn how to use the LOA in order to attract it.

Try to think about all of this in relation to the law of gravity. Newton's first law of motion states that in order for the motion of an object to change, a force must act upon it. If you want to kick a rock across the street, you have to use the force of your leg and foot to make the rock move; otherwise it will stay in the same place. With the LOA, think of the *motion* as an experience. Let us say for example, that you want to experience wealth or you want to attract wealth. In this case the rock, or the object, is wealth. In order to change your experience to attract wealth, a force must act upon it. That force is you. You must make changes to your experience in order to attract wealth. This is the definition of the LOA and illustrates how you can make it work for you (Petocz & Sowey, 2008).

Many people fail to understand or realize that the process of the LOA is not always immediate, and this can lead to unnecessary and premature discouragement. If you go back to our example above, Newton's first law of motion is immediate. If you swing your leg back and kick the rock (assuming the rock's size is small), the rock will immediately move. This is not always the case with the LOA. Some people will start to see results immediately; but for other people it may take years of applying the LOA in order to see results. Although change can happen immediately, the important thing is to remain patient and faithful to the principles of the LOA.

What we outline in this book is what we have found to work for ourselves. The LOA consists of a process where certain steps must be followed in order to get to the next level. The steps are simple, but the process of incorporating the LOA into your life takes time, patience, and effort on your part. Another thing to remember is your faith in the LOA. Make no mistake; fully believing in the LOA is mandatory for success. You are constantly giving off energy with your thoughts, emotions, visualizations, and actions. You must truly believe that the LOA will work for you in order for it to take shape in your life.

Before proceeding with this book, you must be ready to accept the power of the LOA in your life. You must not question whether the LOA will give you what you ask for; you must *know it for a fact* that by making changes in your life and incorporating certain steps, the LOA will begin to manifest in your life.

From this day on, you will want to try to live a life that fully incorporates the LOA. Day by day, you will want to make both small and large changes in your life that will help you move forward with your goal of attracting experiences, concepts, and things into your life. We will give you specific steps to follow in order to do this. More specifically, we will give you six steps that you must follow in order. You must accomplish each step as we have explained them in order to move on to the next.

We also give you broad guidelines to customize the LOA to your individual needs. These guidelines are explained in detail here in order to help you along in the process. No two individuals are the same in this universe, and as such, it is fair to assume that no two people in this universe want to attract the same experiences or things into their lives. Due to this fact, we stick to broad suggestions. The steps that we have outlined in this book are meant to be tailored by you to fit your life and your wants and needs.

The LOA can affect your personal relationships, physical fitness, financial health and medical health. You also have the power to affect every emotion you feel on a daily basis and you have the power to change negative feelings and prolong positive feelings. How you begin your day can make a huge difference in how your day is experienced. If you get out of bed feeling happy and refreshed, you will find that your day will continue on the road to success. Make a point to wake up every single day with a smile on your face and ready to take on anything that comes your way with a positive attitude.

The most important factor for you to realize is that the LOA is real. We use it daily to achieve what we want out of our lives. It exists and it is all around you, so start believing!

Many people may not take the LOA seriously. This is most likely due to either a lack of knowledge or not having been exposed to any success stories about it. Just because you may not understand how a certain set of principles works or why they work, it does not mean the set of principals does not exist. However, there is nothing at all beneficial to gain from assuming there are no positive possibilities that exist today from using the LOA. With that being said, let's get started!

3

What Are Vibrations and Energy?

We are all vibrational beings. You are like a receiving mechanism in that when you set your tuner to a station, you're going to hear what's playing. Whatever you are focused upon is the way you set your tuner, and when you focus there for as little as seventeen seconds, you activate that vibration within you.

> *Once you activate a vibration within you, the Law of Attraction begins responding to that vibration, and you're off and running— whether it's something wanted or unwanted.* (Abraham-Hicks, excerpted from a workshop in North Los Angeles, CA on Sunday, August 18th, 2002)

By now you are probably wondering, what is the actual "law" behind LOA, and how does it operate? Believe it or not, some actual science is attached to the LOA, and it has its roots in theories developed in quantum physics. The word *attraction* comes into play because of the vibrational energy we send to the universe which, seeks out and attracts similar vibrational energy.

Let's take a moment to examine what actually goes on when we use the LOA in our lives. As we mentioned, there are vibrations and energies that correspond to our thoughts and actions. In fact, all of our

thoughts are sending out their own unique energies. Yes, that is correct. Every thought that your mind conjures up is vibrating at its own
frequency and has an impact on the world.

THE ENERGY BEHIND THE LAW OF ATTRACTION

When you think certain thoughts, your brain actually sends out certain electromagnetic waves based on the corresponding frequencies.
When you add your emotions or actions to these vibrations, your
thought vibrations grow even stronger. Thoughts that are coupled
with emotions, and actions are activated to vibrate on a more intense
and powerful level. However, we need to control more than just our
thoughts to produce the results we want via the LOA. It is crucial that
our actions and our emotions also point in the right direction. Real,
guided change can occur when our thoughts, actions, and emotions
are all aligned in a positive direction and their energies compound
with one another.

Let's examine the science behind vibrations and energy for a
moment. All electromagnetic waves have a specific rate or frequency,
which is dependent on movement. You may remember studying wave-
lengths back in high school science class. Often they are represented
by waves like those you would see in the ocean. The actual term
wavelength is the measurement of the distance between one energy
wave crest to the next crest. Electromagnetic waves are described in
terms of energy or frequency. The world is made up of "pulsating
energy," and your thoughts and emotions are part of this energy.
Everything in the world is vibrating and moving. All that we see has
its own vibrational energy pattern. Atoms and subatomic particles
cause different things to resonate different vibrations. Quantum physics, a branch of science unto itself, analyzes how everything in the
world is derived from pure energy at different vibrational levels.

Niels Bohr, the winner of the Nobel Prize in 1922, first stated that
all subatomic particles were actually waveforms. These vibrational
waves are transformed into the physical world we see around us.
Additionally, everything is connected as a vibrational mass of energy.
Bohr realized many truths about how physics works that were previously unrecognized. He was quoted as saying, "If quantum mechanics
hasn't profoundly shocked you, you haven't understood it yet."

Once you realize that you are operating in a larger universe in
which everything is buzzing with its own unique energy, you will
understand why it is so important to control your thoughts and emo-

tions. Each thought you think is almost like a signal to the universe that states, "I want more of this!"

Stop for a moment and ponder the enormity of this statement and its implications. Every thought you have is quite literally a signal being broadcast to the universe requesting and asking that you receive more of whatever it is that you are thinking about. If that doesn't have an impact on your thinking, what does?

Our vibrations can be likened to radio waves. You are broadcasting these vibrations out to the world. Your thoughts and beliefs are broadcast in waves, and once emitted, they join together with additional energy. Your energy waves will seek those that are similar. These join together to form what appearances and events you see in the outside world. This is where the LOA comes in. Viewing our vibrations as radio waves illustrates how the LOA controls your experiences. When you send out your thought (and the powerful energy attached to it), that thought then goes out into the world seeking a match to its vibration. Like attracts like. As we vibrate, we attract what is similar to us.

MESSAGES IN WATER CRYSTALS

Dr. Masaru Emoto is a very interesting person to examine when considering the power of our thoughts and actions over the material world. Dr. Emoto is the author of the *New York Times* best-selling book, *The Hidden Messages of Water.* Believe it or not, this book showed that water could react to our emotions. It chronicles how Dr. Emoto, a Japanese scientist, assembled photographs of crystals that were formed from frozen water. He photographed water that was exposed to different words and emotions. His research documented something very surprising that can actually be seen in those photographs: Positive emotions created showcases of beautiful, magnificent crystals, and negative emotions caused crystals that were malformed and unattractive. Additionally, he found that music could cause changes in the water and its appearance. Beautiful, hopeful, positive music caused the water crystals to look stunning, whereas angry music led to ugly, misshapen crystals.

Emoto's theory is that water can receive an array of emotional frequencies. The universe is made up of seventy percent water, and as a result, our thoughts and emotions can potentially alter and change the world at a level we cannot even begin to comprehend. Dr. Emoto's experiment shows that humans have the ability to change the world through thoughts and emotions.

Another experiment Dr. Emoto tried with water was taping negative and positive messages to the insides of bottles of water. For
example, he taped terms such as *love* and *gratitude* on water bottles
and examining the results. These positive statements corresponded
with the formation of beautiful crystals. Statements such as "You
make me sick" created ugly crystals in the water within the bottle.

Part of what we can take away from this remarkable experiment is
that our negative thoughts have the ability to change our own bodies
and our health. Since the body is also made up of water, we can alter
the wellness and power of our cells through our positive or negative
thinking. We can also impact the wellness of the cells of others. Similarly, there are scientific studies that have looked into the wellness of
plants when people talk to them. Plants that have been told positive
things grow and flourish, while plants that are ignored often wither
and die. This knowledge about plants is so well documented and
established that it is common for even people who are somewhat
skeptical to talk to their plants because doing so produces great
results and healthy, resilient plants.

The thoughts that we think every day have energy that actually sets
up an electromagnetic field around us. We actually attract that which
is equivalent to our vibrations.

ENERGY AND HEALING

Vibrations and energy have been shown to have an incredible ability to heal others as well as ourselves. Some of the numerous energy
healing modalities practiced by people all over the world include
Reiki, Chakra, the Chinese practice of qi gong, and Pranic healing.
The idea behind these healing practices is that our life force (or vibration) has the power to heal. Healers even use the technique of sending
positive and healing energy to others. They may include visualization
in their work—for example, they may visualize that diseased cells
die, or that cells flourish and become healthy.

Energy healing is divided into two categories. Veritable energy
medicine is the label for the types of energy healing that include magnet and light therapy. Energy medicine involving putative energy
fields includes healing techniques such as acupuncture, qi gong, and
Reiki. These modes of healing have been practiced for centuries, with
countless examples of amazing results.

Although many people think that the claim that energy healing
works is unfounded, these theories are, in fact, also supported by ele-

ments of quantum physics. The evolution of the field of quantum physics has proven that the time-space barriers that science previously espoused have been refuted.

In quantum physics, subatomic particles can act on other particles in a way that goes beyond the concepts of Newtonian physics, which is based on the idea that everything revolves around more simple theories of motion. The theories of Newtonian physics are often referred to as classical mechanics.

In fact, many major medical centers are beginning to incorporate alternative medicine techniques based on energy healing into their treatments of patients because studies have shown these treatments to have positive results. Although major hospitals are reluctant to agree to use energy healing modalities, the results that have been seen in patients have shown a very large body of evidence that energy healing techniques work. Because positive results in so many patients are undeniable, these institutions often have no choice but to offer these alternative healing options to their patients. After all, doctors are required to take the Hippocratic Oath in which they promise to do everything they can to act in the best interest of the patient's health and well-being. If energy healing produces results (which it does), doctors often feel they have no choice but to offer these types of treatments in addition to the traditional types.

In sum, vibrations and energy have powerful implications for both science and medicine. We have the ability to affect and alter our vibrations on a personal level to bring about change in our lives and the lives of others. As soon as most people become aware of this fact, they begin to work hard to monitor and shift their ideas and actions on a daily basis. This is the beginning of allowing the LOA to bring positive results into your world.

THINK THE TRUTH, DESPITE APPEARANCES

When you break it down, your thoughts are nothing more than a unique pattern of energy you have created. When you change that pattern, you begin to bring new experiences and thoughts to yourself. Your thoughts, feelings, and actions have a magnetic effect in the world.

Have you ever had a day where everything went great for no reason at all? Have you ever had a day where everything went horribly wrong for no reason at all? Most of us dismiss this as the laws of probability, luck, or chance. But what if it goes deeper than that? What if it's the

LOA at work? How about a series of unexplained coincidences? Have you ever thought randomly about a friend who you haven't seen in twenty years, only to have him/her appear hours later or call you soon after? Most people, even those who do not necessarily believe in the LOA, have reported that sort of experience, but they chalk it up to coincidence. Yet, when many people around the world are reporting such an experience with great frequency, it begins to look like more than just random chance.

The truth is the odds are potentially astronomical that this sort of circumstance is based on chance (we say potentially astronomical because, if you live in a small town or have stayed in the same area where the person in question once lived, the odds may be a bit better). However, what if you moved thousands of miles away and have not thought of or seen a person in years, and he then appears in your life? The feeling can be eerie enough to indeed seem as though some other force is at play, no matter how much of a skeptic you may be.

To varying degrees, we have experiences like this all the time and often dismiss them as meaningless. Why do we dismiss experiences that are clearly not possibly random? The truth is that society tends to condition people to dismiss such occurrences as chance mostly because, until recently, to do otherwise would conflict with many of the notions of modern science. In the past, and not that distant a past at that, discussing that you were experiencing such a phenomenon would have been enough to find yourself being accused of being insane. Many people reporting similar phenomena were also accused of being in league with demons or were quickly labeled as witches. Accordingly, people began to systematically dismiss such events as random chance in order to avoid being an outcast. However, as more principles of science begin to be understood and our knowledge continues to grow, the status quo of accepting previously unacceptable coincidences is also changing.

The importance of social pressure in being able to make us deny what is evident and apparent to our own senses should not be dismissed lightly. Social institutions and pressures have been used expertly for generations to affect how people think, what they believe, and yes, even how they perceive the world, the universe, and their place in it. Social pressure is a seriously powerful tool that historically has been used more for suppression and oppression than expression.

Just because the popular and cultivated opinions of the day do not agree with a certain set of beliefs does not mean that those beliefs are not truthful. One commonly cited example is that of people in ancient times believing that the world was flat. Then, seemingly miraculously at the time, it was discovered that the world was in fact round. However, many people continued to believe that the world was flat even after overwhelming and extreme evidence to the contrary for a very long time afterward. It took many years, but as you now know, the currently accepted theory is that the world is indeed round. We laugh now at the mere idea that the world could be flat in the same way that years ago people scoffed at the notion that the world could be round. We hope to illustrate that it is in this same way that science eventually could come full circle and the theories that are currently thought of as alternative could eventually become mainstream.

Great minds throughout history have been persecuted, tortured, and even murdered because they defied the popularly held beliefs of the day. It helps to view all of this in context because, though others may not believe that the LOA works or that there exists science that can directly verify its validity, doesn't mean that you should go along with them or doubt the veracity of the LOA.

Wallace Wattle's classic book, *The Science of Getting Rich*, was originally written in 1910 and is one of the earliest and most widely read books about the LOA. He writes, "To think according to appearances is easy; to think truth regardless of appearances is laborious and requires the expenditure of more power than any other work we are called upon to perform." His words still ring quite true 100 years later.

Where the LOA is concerned, the word *courage* is often overlooked. However, it should be noted that often it takes great courage to see beyond what the ill-informed mind and its limited perception sees and follow a different path. Getting whatever it is that you want out of life takes courage. It is often not easy to reach beyond day-to-day outward appearances and grasp the truth beyond.

The key to getting what you want is to cause a shift in your vibrations to what you do want. That is why it is significant to change your thoughts and ideas from negative ones that you want to avoid to positive ones that reflect what you want. If you are always seeking the best and most positive thoughts, you will then attract the events and situations that are more similar to what you want. Another more objective way to look at this might be: Shouldn't you want to be thinking the most positive thoughts possible? Why wouldn't you want to be thinking thoughts that make you happy? The truth is that there is no logical reason for you to want to have anything other than uplifting and positive thoughts. However, because you are not a machine, your thoughts are unlikely to be positive all the time. Human emotions run the gamut, and it is and will be a challenge at times to focus solely on positive thoughts. Even the most intelligent and enlightened among us will have a difficult time thinking positive thoughts on certain occasions. However, we implore you not to get discouraged if and when you find yourself having trouble or reverting to negative thoughts. Simply learn to recognize when you are doing so, and refocus on the positive. With continual practice, you will have a much easier time doing this.

If society has conditioned us to believe that so many of the unusual and extraordinary things we see are just random background noise, the same can be said for how we think. Society often mocks happy people as being foolish, misguided, and naïve. However, those people who are always happy-go-lucky see the bright side of life and receive many positive benefits to their lives as a result.

Modern medical science is proving that happy people often live longer than those with a more negative view (Veenhoven et al., 2008). Optimistic people have been shown to deal with life's setbacks better and are generally healthier. Western medicine's early theory that the mind and body are completely unconnected has been eroded considerably.

It is counterproductive to succumb to societal pressures or believe people who tell you it is foolish to always think happy thoughts. As we have discussed, your thoughts, and their amazing significance and impact on your life, are the only things that you can control absolutely and consistently. It is beneficial to your life in countless ways to strive to think positive and uplifting thoughts as much as possible.

The simple act of being and thinking positively can affect your life in some very practical ways. For example, who would you rather be around, a positive person or a negative person? Some people may prefer to be around a negative person for more of the time. Imagine how this affects the LOA! It's simply illogical to seek out people who do not fit with your own personal goals of success and happiness (assuming, of course, that those are your goals, since you are reading this book). Through being positive and seeking out the company of others who are positive and optimistic, you are increasing the chances of the LOA working for you.

Positive people as companions are much more likely to feel that your goals, dreams and desires are possible and support you in achieving them. What would you rather hear, "I bet you're right, I bet that will work" or "That is probably impossible, maybe you should reconsider"? On occasion, of course, an idea might be actually be dangerous, but for the most part, most of us would want to be around the person that says, "I bet that will work." Even better, let's hope this optimistic person offers to help!

If you really take a few moments to think it over, you are likely to conclude that you want to be around people who give off "good vibrations." After all, what good can really come from spending your time around negative people? Your life should be very important to you, and you should not let just anyone drift in and out of it. A smart person realizes that his friends and acquaintances directly affect what he is able to attract to his life. Where the LOA is concerned, it pays to be selective and seek out all the good vibrations that you can find.

The universe is always delivering the vibrations you send out to some other part of the universe. Unfortunately, we cannot just hide out or take a break and not send energetic signals out. Again, that is why doing all that you can to control your thoughts and emotions is so significant. This point cannot be stressed enough. Additionally, there are different levels and intensities of vibration. The higher the frequency of vibration you send out, the greater the force. More passion around a thought or emotion creates more of that energy. Passion seems to attract more energy to thoughts.

Have you ever noticed that people who have intense, dynamic personalities and are full of ideas, passions, and enthusiasm always seem to be having dynamic and interesting things happen to them? On the other hand, people who tend to be more dull and unenthusiastic tend to not experience as much excitement or as many extraordinary events in their lives. It is obviously important to monitor and control the vibrations we are sending out. Luckily, we have a gauge that we carry around with us that lets us know information and details about our vibrations. That wonderful and accurate gauge is our emotions.

If you are seeking to learn what kind of vibrations you are sending out and what types of experiences and events you should be expecting, just check your emotions. If you are feeling positive, you know you are a vibrational match for what you want. Any negative thoughts or feelings should be signals that you are out of alignment with what you want to achieve. It is of crucial importance to monitor your feelings very carefully. They will let you know when you are drawing good things to yourself and when you are off-track. Your emotions will not deceive you, and they will always reflect the truth back to you in a highly accurate manner.

4

Step One: Changing Negative Powers into Positive Powers

Welcome to the first of the six steps of *You Can Attract It*. These steps are going to tell you how you can prepare yourself for success by incorporating the LOA into your life. While reading these steps, we encourage you to keep an open mind because that is what abundance is all about.

Now that you know what the LOA is, how do you put it to use? The key to using the LOA is within your four powers: your thoughts, emotions, visualizations, and actions. You have an incredible capacity for thoughts and emotions; these are truly endless. In this chapter, we will go into detail about your four powers. We refer to them as powers because they each have the power to change your life dramatically. When you change all four and allow them to work for you, you will have created a strong foundation for the benefits of the LOA in your life.

YOUR THOUGHTS

Throughout your day, week, month, or year, you have thoughts running through your mind. Actually it is estimated that you have sixteen thousand thoughts every single day. Guess what? You are in control of these thoughts. You might be thinking, *How can I possibly be in charge of that many thoughts a day?* The answer is because both your conscious and your subconscious are always active.

Let us start with your thoughts. Ask yourself: Do I have complete control of my thoughts? Your answer is probably no, but with time and practice, you can. Your spouse is not in control of your thoughts, nor are your boss, your friends, your family, or anyone else. You are the only person who can be in control and change the way you think.

The reason it is so important to be in control of your thoughts is because they shape who you are and your perspective on life. It has been shown that negative thoughts can lead to anxiety (Muris, Mayer, den Adel, Roos, & van Wamelen, 2009). What you are thinking right now, in the present, will shape your future through the LOA. If you are thinking happy and positive thoughts right now, the LOA will bring more happy and positive thoughts to you in the future.

The biggest hurdle you will face with the LOA is changing your negative thoughts into positive ones. This process will take time, patience, and practice. However, it is the single most important thing you can do in order to be successful with the LOA. Once you master this skill, your positive thoughts will begin to manifest and bring great things into your life. A positive thought is many times more powerful than a single negative thought. If you replace one negative thought with a positive one, you are going to feel great things begin to take shape. If you replace *all* of your negative thoughts...imagine the possibilities!

CHANGING NEGATIVE THOUGHTS INTO POSITIVE THOUGHTS

In order to change your negative thoughts into positive thoughts, you first have to be aware of your thoughts. What are you thinking? You may be reading a book, but are you focusing on the words you are reading, or is your mind wandering to something else? This happens all the time—we tend to zone out and think about something without even being aware of it.

The first step in changing negative thoughts to positive thoughts is targeting your negative thoughts. To do this, you must first learn which thoughts are negative. For example, you might be thinking, *I forgot to take out the trash this morning. How could I be so forgetful?*

This is clearly a negative thought, and you are putting yourself down by calling yourself forgetful, which does not accomplish anything. You are telling the universe that you are forgetful and cannot keep up with simple chores. When you realize you are thinking a negative thought such as the one above, you must literally tell yourself, "This is a negative thought; how can I change it into a positive one?" You must then think of a positive thought to replace the negative one. For example, you can think, *I forgot to take out the trash this morning. That's okay, everyone makes mistakes. I will take it out when I get home this evening.*

Now this was a simple example. It was easy to tell that the above was a negative thought. Not all negative thoughts are easy to turn around, but it is very important to do so. For example, let's say that you are at work and you hear a co-worker talking negatively about your performance. It will probably seem natural for you to either be hard on yourself or angry at your co-worker, or maybe both. However, neither is constructive and neither will attract positive things into your life. What you must do is turn the negative thought into a positive one, or even better, think positively before a negative thought has time to form. In this case, you will want to think, *She is right, I did not perform very well on that task, I will try harder from now on. I am capable of going above and beyond.* Or, *I tried my hardest, I worked very hard and I am very pleased with my performance.*

Now you have learned the importance of targeting negative thoughts and changing them into positive ones. At first, it might be best for you to write your negative thoughts down. On the following page, is a sample worksheet you can use to write down negative thoughts in the left-hand column and in the right-hand column, turn that thought into a positive one. You will want to do this with all of your negative thoughts, as writing them down will help you decide how to turn them into positive thoughts.

Use this worksheet for a week or however long you need to until you get the hang of this exercise. You'll know you have mastered this skill when you notice that you can immediately change them in your head without writing them down.

THE POWER OF POSITIVE THINKING

When you master the skill of changing negative thoughts into positive ones, the next step is to try to not allow any negative thoughts to

Negative Thoughts	Positive Thoughts

pop up in your mind at all. Mastery of this skill will come with time and patience. You will notice that negative thoughts will become less frequent; instead, only positive thoughts will exist in your mind. We feel it helps to think about it this way: Thoughts have a frequency. A positive thought has a higher frequency than a negative thought. The universe hears a higher frequency or higher vibration and gives back things that also have higher frequencies. When the universe hears a low frequency or low vibration, it continues to deliver other negative things. You must strive to give off a high frequency and a high vibration at all times. When you notice yourself putting less effort into containing negative thoughts and having less negative thoughts altogether, you know you are on the right path. The LOA rewards positive thinking with positive things and positive actions.

YOUR EMOTIONS

It helps to make the distinction that your feelings and emotions are different from your thoughts in that thoughts create feelings. Some people might have an easier time pinpointing feelings rather than thoughts. However, both your thoughts and your feelings are very important aspects of the LOA. You must be aware of your feelings and whether they are positive or negative. Negative feelings do not empower you. Your goal is to get rid of negative feelings and replace them with positive ones, feelings that empower you and bring you joy and happiness.

Your feelings have a lot to do with who you are and what kinds of vibrations you are putting out there—not only to the people around you, but also to the universe. What are you feeling right now? Perhaps you have negative feelings right now, such as feeling tired, lazy, depressed, worthless, jealous, frustrated, or worried. Maybe you have positive feelings right now, such as optimism, hopefulness, joy, love, enthusiasm, passion, or belief. Evaluate how you are feeling right now. You know the difference between feeling happy and feeling depressed.

Whatever you are feeling, realize that it consumes you. Whether positive or negative, your feelings consume your mind, body and spirit, and it is up to you (and only you) to try to improve your feelings or maintain positive feelings. In order to make the LOA work for you, you should strive to be aware of your feelings at all times. Remember that *why* you are feeling a negative feeling is not important in this context. Defending negative emotions will get you nowhere. There is no good reason for you to keep feeling a negative emotion. You must leave all excuses, defenses, and reasons for them at the door. You deserve happiness. You deserve to feel good at all times. Remember this always.

CHANGING NEGATIVE EMOTIONS INTO POSITIVE EMOTIONS

Changing negative feelings into positive feelings is similar to changing your thoughts, but with feelings, you can start feeling good right away, even if those feelings have not quite manifested. You are in control of changing your negative emotions into positive ones. The first step is to target your emotions. How do you feel? Try to ask yourself this question several times a day, not only when you feel really good or really bad. Be aware of your emotions, as they affect you on many levels. Your emotions determine your vibrations, and your vibrations are how you speak to the universe. If you are feeling down, you get back from the universe what you are feeling. You will get a whole lot of negativity back into your life. You do not want that!

Listed below is an emotional graph that you can use to target your feelings. The emotions listed at the top give out high frequencies. If you are feeling these emotions, it means you are connected with the universe. Conversely, the ones on the bottom disengage you from the universe and give out low vibrations.

1. Empowerment
2. Enthusiasm
3. Hopefulness
4. Contentment
5. Boredom
6. Disappointment
7. Worry
8. Anger
9. Insecurity
10. Disempowerment

Use this scale to grade where your emotions stand. If you are somewhere between boredom and contentment, you would be a 4.5. Your goal is to move up the scale. In order to change your negative feelings into positive feelings you must bring forth thoughts that improve the way you are feeling. For example, to bring you from boredom to contentment, what kind of thoughts would have to be present to create this change? Hopefully you are not bored reading this book, but if you are feeling bored, you can think, *I am pleased with what I am reading.* This will help you reach contentment. To go from contentment to hopefulness, you can think, *I am going to learn great things from this book.* Do you see the pattern? You are moving up the scale by changing your thoughts and feeling the improvement that comes with doing so. To go from hopefulness to enthusiasm, you can think to yourself, *I cannot wait to keep reading the rest of this book, I am learning so much.* And finally, to reach empowerment, you can think, *I can truly change my life with these techniques. I am empowered by the Law of Attraction.* With this example it is important to not just think these thoughts but to recognize and really feel the corresponding feelings with the thoughts. You cannot pretend to feel something. You must truly feel the emotion in order to create the vibration. This process will take practice and some time to master, but we encourage you to do this whenever you want or need to improve your emotions.

On the following page, we have included a worksheet to help you change your negative emotions into positive ones. The left-hand column is for listing your current state of emotion. It can be any emotion, even if it is not on the list above. Write it down, and then on the right-hand column, write a statement that improves your overall emotional state. For example: You are feeling disappointed about not getting a call back from someone. You would write "disappointed" in the left-hand column. In the right-hand column, you can write, "I am sure she is just busy, she will get back to me when she can." Then, you can write "hopefulness." You are hopeful that the person will call you back. In just one minute, you went from feeling disappointed to feeling hopeful.

By doing this, whether you have to work at it or not, you have improved your emotional state and you are giving off higher vibrations. Feeling hopeful puts high vibrations out to the universe and makes it more likely that the universe will pay attention to your vibrations and the woman will call you back. This is how the LOA works when you develop the ability to change your negative feelings into positive ones.

THE POWER OF POSITIVE EMOTIONS

We hope that you are realizing just how powerful your emotions can be in your life. This all has to do with the LOA and how simple

Current State of Emotion	Improved Thought/ New Emotional State

changes in the way you feel can have a direct effect in your life and in the universe. The universe will reward you when you start having true positive emotions and feelings toward the things you want in your life.

You, your emotions, and the LOA are all connected. This is why you want positive emotions, because of course you want the LOA to give you positive things in your life. Positive emotions make you feel good. You should always strive to feel good. You should want to feel good at all times and you deserve to feel good at all times.

Positive emotions also create desire. Desire comes from the awareness of new possibilities. Desire means you look toward your future and see that it is bright. You must be steadfast in knowing that the future will bring positive steadfast energy into your life. If you continue to feel uncertain of your future in any way, you are not creating positive vibrations for the universe and the LOA will not work.

VISUALIZATION

In addition to thoughts and emotions, we as humans also have visualization. We see things in our minds and imagine things. For the LOA to work for you, it is very helpful to incorporate visualization into your life.

The following is a simple visualization exercise. Read the following passage and as you do, try to immerse yourself in the words and picture the scene in your mind as clearly as possible:

> As I stand on the beach, my senses come alive and I notice every detail around me. I look at the white sandy beach to my left and right, and it seems to go on forever in both directions. I look out at the water. There are little waves coming toward me. I look at the color of the water; it is brilliant blue. There is water as far as my eyes can see. I look up at the sky and notice seagulls flying above. I can hear their calls to one another. I notice how they glide in the air so effortlessly. I walk closer to the water. I am at the water's edge. I feel the water surround my feet and ankles. The water is warm and refreshing. I wiggle my toes in the sand; it feels good on my bare feet. I take a little while to listen to the soft sounds of the waves breaking on the shore. Every wave I see rolling in toward me relaxes me even more. I take a deep breath in and smell the salty air. It smells clean and pure. I am completely at ease. I decide to take a little walk down the beach. I walk very slowly, enjoying every step that I take. I am at complete peace here on the beach. I continue to walk. There is no one on this beach

except me. I feel very comfortable here. As I walk, I bend down and pick up a shell. It is pink and white. I run my fingers around it, and it is smooth on one side and bumpy on the other. I put it to my ear and I can hear the sound of the ocean. I put the shell back on the beach and continue my walk.

Pause for a moment to assess your feelings after reading this passage. This story involved all of your senses—sight, smell, taste, hearing, touch. The more senses a story involves, the easier it is to get wrapped up in it. The more details there are, the more thought it takes to imagine it. The more thought it takes to picture the story, the more emotion you put into it. This is an important trick in using the LOA. Just like your thoughts and feelings attract things, so does visualization. You picture yourself doing things in your mind all the time. Maybe you think about going to the grocery store, and the first image that pops up in your mind is picking up an apple at the produce department. Just like you are in charge of your thoughts and emotions, you are in charge of your visual field and imagination. Use it to help create positive thoughts and send positive vibrations to the universe.

CHANGING NEGATIVE IMAGES INTO POSITIVE IMAGES

If you frequently picture negative images in your mind, you need to first be aware of this and then start changing negative images into positive ones. Having negative images in your mind or imagining negative past events only leads to stress and more negative images. It is important to be aware of the visualizations you have in your mind at any time. For example, at some point in your life, you have probably shown a negative emotion of anger and/or jealousy and wished someone did not exist. Perhaps you imagined life without that person. These are negative images, and you must remove them from your mind's eye. Negative images and visualizations only tell the universe to put more negativity back into your life, and that is not what you want.

When you catch yourself picturing something negative, immediately remove the negative image and focus on something positive. A great technique to use in this situation is to picture yourself in a beautiful and calm place such as a mountain or the beach. The key here is to distract yourself from the negative image and imagine something positive instead. This will take a little practice at first, but you will get better at it and the process will become easier with practice.

THE POWER OF VISUALIZATION

You might be wondering how visualization ties in with the LOA on a deeper level. Later, when we talk more in detail about achieving exactly what you want with the LOA, you will have to visualize the things you want. For example, if you want a better job that pays more money, you will want to visualize this better job. You will want to imagine going to this job every day. You will picture yourself there and see the details of your clothing. You will see your boss or you will see that you are the boss and you see all of your employees. You will imagine getting a large paycheck every week. Do you see where we are going with this? Just like in the story above, when we asked you to immerse yourself in images, you will want to visually immerse yourself in all the details of whatever it is that you want.

The first thing we want to focus on is the importance of imagining yourself already having what you want. We are going to use the example of better cars because this is something that we the authors both wanted in the past. We pictured ourselves already having the cars we wanted. On a day-to-day basis, as much as humanly possible, we constantly envisioned already having new cars, driving them, what it felt like to drive the new car, and what it smelled like to have them; we envisioned every detail of the cars we wanted.

Go ahead and picture one of the things that you want. Picture it with as many details as possible. Imagine yourself surrounded by it, in it, or achieving it. Imagine yourself "in the moment" in possession of one of the things you have been wanting. Revisit this vision several times a day. This is a way of reminding yourself of and reinforcing what you are working for and what you are changing your life for. Let your visions be a motivator. You must try to be patient while you wait for the LOA to come into your life. Keep your vision strong by thinking about it daily. Great things will come to you.

Envisioning the things you want is a hugely important step to take in order to attract whatever it is that you want. You may be saying to yourself right now, "How is that possible? How can I already envision whatever I want?" Learn everything there is to know about what you are asking for. Know all the details about what you are asking for. Know how it will make you feel. Know what it looks like. Know what it smells like. Know how it feels. You should realize all of this without even having it yet.

Visualization of the things you want should optimally occur several times a day for at least a minute at a time. When you imagine these things in your head, you are again giving off vibrations that are telling the universe what you want. Picture your dream house and what it looks like from the outside and what it feels like to be inside. Imagine what the view is from a window. Imagine cooking in the kitchen, walking up the stairs, and leaving in your car from the garage. Immerse yourself in your visualizations as much as possible. What does the house smell like? What color are the floors? You want to picture all the details and make it real as possible in your head.

Another helpful approach is to pretend you are painting a picture of what you want in your head. Creative visualization takes a little practice at first, but it is very powerful in the LOA. If you have trouble with it at first, it might help you to write down what you want and then picture it in your mind. Each time you think of that specific thing you want, add more detail to it. Make it almost life-like in your mind. Visualization is a very powerful technique.

YOUR ACTIONS

In getting the most out of the LOA, along with your thoughts, feelings, and images, there are also your actions to consider. Your actions must be in alignment with the universe to allow the things you want to come to you and for the LOA to work for you. Positive actions create vibrations, just like positive thoughts do. At the core of your actions is your well-being. Everything that you do is to improve your well-being.

Your actions toward yourself are also extremely important. They affect all of your experiences in life, including your relationships with other people, your ability to accumulate wealth, and your health. We want you to make positive actions and choices in your life because positive actions lead to receiving more positive experiences into your life.

It is important to make the distinction that in relation to actions, we are not talking about how your actions affect other people in your life. We are talking about how the choices you make affect you both in your current state and your future. The LOA is all about you. You must focus on treating yourself with respect and loving yourself, and the universe will give love and respect back to you in many various forms and experiences. If there was ever a time to be selfish and completely focus on you, this is it!

CHANGING NEGATIVE ACTIONS INTO POSITIVE ACTIONS

There are three key positive actions that you must try to create from current negative actions. These negative actions prevent the LOA from working for you, and instead, these negative actions are working against you. You must attempt to totally eliminate negative actions and negative thoughts about what you can (or cannot) accomplish and start incorporating powerful, positive actions into your everyday life. It is important to point out here that these are conceptual actions. We are preparing you for steps later in this book where you will actually have to take action. But for right now, we want you to change your attitude about the actions you are going to take in the near future.

The first negative action that you must change is not asking for what you want. Maybe you are not asking for what you want because you do not know what you want. Or it may be the case that you are not asking for what you want because you feel like you do not deserve it. The reason is not important. Remember, excuses and the reasons behind them do not create positive vibrations with the LOA. You must get rid of any analytical mindset and instead focus on what you do want. The opposite, positive action is to ask for what you want. We are writing this book to tell you that you deserve great things in your life. You are a strong being who may not know exactly what you want yet, but you must have confidence in yourself that you will soon figure it out with the help of Step Three and then learn how to ask for it in Step Four.

The second negative action is not allowing the LOA to work for you. You are probably not aware that you are not allowing positive energy into your life. Your actions may be preventing good from happening in your life. Again, the reasons why you are preventing good things from occurring in your life are not important. What is important is that you let go of this barrier. It is as if you have a wall up and are fighting against the universe. You must tear this wall down. Once you tear the wall down, there will be nothing between you and your allowing positive things into your life, and the LOA will start working for you. The opposite, positive action is to allow good things to enter your life. We will provide more instruction on allowing the LOA to work for you in Step Five of this book.

The third and last negative action is pushing against receiving good things and experiences in your life. In other words, you may sabotage yourself without knowing it. Good things may be very close to entering your life, or may actually enter your life, but you push them away. This happens to many people in relationships, for example. They are scared to accept a loving and committed relationship, so they push it away. The person they push away could make them happy, but they will never know because they work against it.

This also occurs when a goal of reaching success or wealth is pushed away by the fear of success or the fear of failure. There is no need to be fearful of success or failure. People who are scared of failure or success usually fall somewhere in the middle, never completely allowing themselves to receive success into their life but never actually failing either. The important thing here is to realize that you *can* be a success. Your positive actions and positive experiences will lead to great things happening in your life with the LOA. The opposite of pushing it away is the positive action of receiving it and being thankful for it.

THE POWER OF POSITIVE ACTIONS

Replacing negative actions with positive actions creates vibrations and connects you with the universe. Positive actions are more powerful and create good things and experiences in your life. The good created by positive actions is much more powerful than negative actions. Good is always stronger and more powerful than bad. Positive actions bring a constant flow of positive energy into every aspect of your life. When you ask, allow, and receive good things in your life, you open the door to unlimited happiness. However, you must be intentional in your good actions. The power of your positive actions is a force greater than you can fathom.

5

The Power of Appreciation

"The more gratefully we fix our minds on the Supreme when good things come to us, the more good things we will receive, and the more rapidly they will come; and the reason simply is that the mental attitude of gratitude draws the mind into closer touch with the source from which the blessings come."

—Wallace D. Wattles, *The Science of Getting Rich*

One of the most powerful tools we can use to activate the LOA in our life is to practice appreciation of what we already have and everything around us. When we experience and cultivate feelings of appreciation, we are informing the universe that we already have what we want. Experiencing feelings of appreciation is one of the fastest ways of getting the LOA to work on your behalf.

In previous chapters, we discussed exercises for bringing happiness into your life. Focusing on experiencing emotions of appreciation is a key path to follow for cultivating happiness and abundance in your life. Positive statements of affirmation, for example, are a great method by which to appreciate your life and expand your happiness. Even if your life isn't the way you would ideally want it to be, there is still plenty to appreciate and be grateful for. The goal of experiencing the power of appreciation is to focus on what you do have already in your life in order to shift your focus away from lack. It is important to draw on feelings that support abundance. After all, if what you are seeking in your life is abundance, it makes sense to focus on the abundance of what you already have. This is the groundwork through which you can effectively use the techniques we have discussed in this book—visualization, asking for what you want, taking positive action, and receiving from the universe.

You may doubt that there is abundance for you to be thankful of, but it's true. You may be reading this book, thinking *I am poor,* or *I have little going for me.* Perhaps you feel as though your future is bleak, and you have experienced many disappointments in life thus far. However, keep in mind that odds are, if you have the time to read this book, you are better off than the vast majority of humanity. You can first be thankful for the ability to read. It may also help to consider that most humans today simply do not have much in the way of free time or material resources. In fact, many of us in the world are poor and lack many of life's most basic necessities, such as food, clean water and housing. Most of us sadly forget that every day on this planet people are starving, and in fact, every day, scores of people die because they do not have food. Others die from poor sanitation. If you have enough to eat, clean water, and a roof over your head, you are very lucky indeed.

So Much to Appreciate about the Present

Often the past is glamorized as being a wonderful place where everything was simpler and purer. While there are exceptions, on the whole this is simply not true. You may have heard, for example, that the average Roman citizen died by the age of twenty-eight or some other similar story. Though today we do not perceive twenty-eight as being "old," only a couple of thousand years ago, twenty-eight was way "over the hill." The elite upper class may have still seen their 60s, 70s, 80s, and even on occasion their 90s, but for the average person, death came quickly and early.

Today, virtually all of the most educated people who have ever lived are currently alive. There are more brilliant minds alive today by far than at any other time in history. Diseases are being better managed and cured at a fantastic rate. New technologies in every field are seeing breakthroughs almost daily. And the speed at which these discoveries are taking place is, itself, quickening. Consider what life looked like sixty years ago. So much of what modern life consists of was then only a dream of science fiction. It is almost certain that you live in the single most exciting time in human history. There are medical breakthroughs occurring daily that will almost certainly extend your life, perhaps even very significantly.

If this seems unlikely to you, consider how much medical technology has advanced in just the last twenty years, not to mention the last forty. The medical technology of forty years ago seems absolutely primitive by today's standards. Nanomedicine promises to repair damage at the cellular level; organ printing (a technology similar to your home printer) will literally print new organs that your body will not reject; and a cure for cancer is likely around the corner. These are all breakthroughs that most of us will live to see. The odds are good that if you are reading this book, you will live longer than anyone thought you could when you were born.

Appreciate the fact that leading scientists feel that we are only a few years away from finding life in space. It sounds absurd, but scientists at SETI (Search for Extraterrestrial Intelligence), which searches for life in space, believe that within twenty years, we will not only find life in space, but intelligent life. More than likely you will be alive for this announcement. Even with all the problems that the world has, even with all of its chaos, you will likely live to see the announcement that life, and perhaps even intelligent life, has been found in space. Even today, as we write this book, it looks very likely that there is simple microbial life on Mars.

The bottom line is that there are so many new technologies headed our way that the future is bound to be amazing beyond most of our dreams. Even just 100 years ago, most people spent their entire lives on farms working the land on which they were born. Most people received very little education and knew very little about the world. Much of the world is still like this today, but there is also a sea of rapid, never before seen change. As more people are exposed to more knowledge and more education, many of today's seemingly daunting problems will crumble beneath the tidal wave of human ingenuity. The future is not going to be perfect, but it is certainly going to be interesting.

With humanity coming out of its infancy, there will be many wonders to witness. You are lucky enough to be alive for the show. Your experience is likely to be so much richer than that of the average person living just 100 years ago. Don't lose the importance of this point—you have much to appreciate. Remember, *you* control your life and you can chart any course you wish to take.

BREAK THE CYCLE OF LACKING APPRECIATION

When we feel significant emotional highs and happiness for what we have in our lives, we effectively send out a signal to the universe that we want more of what we are experiencing. Consequently, the universe will send back more to be grateful for. Similarly, when we send out feelings and thoughts of distress or lack of what we want, the universe will match those thoughts and feelings as well.

Since part of the equation in getting the LOA to work for our benefit is to act as though we already have the success we are seeking, it is very important to practice experiencing feelings of appreciation for your life and all that you already have. We have to remember that in each minute of our lives we are already experiencing great abundance. Remember to be thankful for each passing moment. You likely are familiar with the adage that we live in the present, and the reason it is called the *present* is that each passing moment is a gift. This saying, while often overused, actually holds a great deal of truth.

If you are feeling frustrated and angry about a situation in your life, start taking some time to appreciate how lucky you are to even have this situation. With a little analysis, on most occasions you will have to admit that you are lucky to have had the problem in the first place. For example, did you have a data crash and lose your computer files? Take a moment and reflect on how lucky you are to even have a computer. Did you arrive late to an appointment? Take a moment to appreciate how minor a setback this incident likely is in the grand scheme of things.

Always focusing on what there is to be grateful for is something that you need to make a habit of in order to make the LOA work to its full effectiveness in your life. After all, your mind may be, in a sense, addicted to thinking and perceiving negative thoughts. Like breaking any addiction, it is necessary to set up a pattern of positive progress toward breaking the addiction and its grasp over you. Since your brain is accustomed to thinking the same kinds of thoughts and experiencing the same types of emotions in a specific manner, it actually has set up neurological pathways through which your thinking manifests. These are the channels of thinking that your brain is used to; however, they might not be the best ways of thinking. As a result, thinking these negative thoughts may actually be your comfort level.

As an example, you can compare your dependence and comfort with negative thinking to an alcoholic who has had six beers every day for the last ten years. In the case of the alcoholic, drinking—as well as the feelings and thoughts that the drinking sets into motion— are an addiction for this person. Similarly, your negative thoughts and brainwaves that these ideas set up also have an addictive quality. Of course, not everyone is an alcoholic, but many people have some minor addictions in their lives they can relate this to. For example, perhaps you may be addicted to eating doughnuts or going out for pizza. These are things you know you shouldn't do because these foods are unhealthy in excess, but perhaps you don't resist the temptation. Many people find that their bodies crave these foods, and consequently, their actions guide them to eat unhealthy meals. Similarly, your brain may be addicted to thinking negative thoughts and maintaining negative beliefs in a habitual fashion.

In order to change, you actually need to retrain your mind to think and believe with a new pattern. Once you have established a new pattern, your positive thoughts and beliefs will seem far more commonplace. Thinking thoughts that incorporate appreciation and love will start to be your new comfort level.

HOW TO MANIFEST MORE ABUNDANCE THROUGH APPRECIATION

One of the ways to reprogram your mind to incorporate new and positive thoughts of abundance is to set up a gratitude journal or gratitude list. This practice has been useful to many people. For this exercise, you simply make a list of all of the things you are thankful for in your life. You can start by committing to listing a set number of items you are grateful for. For example, you could commit to writing five, ten, or fifteen things you are grateful for each day. You can achieve that many grateful thoughts each day if you wish. It is all within your reach. Some people create lists of hundreds of things they are grateful for each day. We suggest starting with as many as you are comfortable with or can think of.

You may want to go out and get a nice bound book or dedicated notebook to use for your list. Perhaps you may feel more comfortable typing your list on the computer before you get started with your workday. The important thing is to remember to get into a set routine of writing these items down. This practice is what will retrain and reposition your old thoughts into new thoughts of abundance.

It is suggested that you make your list of gratitudes in the morning, as this exercise can yield positive results by shifting your thinking into that of positivity and abundance early in the day. This is a great way to reposition your day shortly after you wake up. As a result, you very well might attract abundant thoughts and experiences throughout the day as you go about your tasks. Some people also choose to write their gratitude list before they go to sleep for the night so that they can comprehensively write down everything that happened that particular day that they are grateful for.

At first you may find that you are having trouble coming up with grateful thoughts and feelings to add to your list. It is important to remember that with practice, making these lists will become easier and easier for you. The truth in the old saying "practice makes perfect" holds true here. The more you focus on adding to the list and feeling these emotions of appreciation, the more easily ideas will flow freely to you for your list.

If you are having trouble getting started with your gratitude list, simply begin by including the basic things you have around you. You can start with even the smallest things to be grateful for in your life. Even if you have no money, and everything around you seems to be falling apart, there is *something* to be grateful for. Even if it is water or air that you can truly feel thankful for, that is enough of a start for the list to get your energies flowing in the right direction.

Here is an example of what your list may look like:

Things I Am Grateful for Today

I am grateful that I have food in my refrigerator

I am grateful to have a place to live

I am grateful that I have clean water to drink

I am grateful I have this computer to write my list

The above is just an example of what a gratitude list could look like. Of course, feel free to include what inspires you to feel good. Your list can be more creative if you wish. As you right your path, you will find your list growing more in-depth and begin to include a wider range of emotions and insights for what you appreciate about life and your world. It is up to you list anything you want on your gratitude list. Remember the list is meant for you to bring more positive energies and emotions into your life.

CREATING NEW HABITS

By focusing on the items that we are thankful for, we increase the power and activate more of the good in life. Simply note these good, positive events and experiences as they occur in your journal. Soon you will notice that there are more and more positive events and experiences to focus upon. When experiences happen to you that you do not desire, shift your focus to something good about the situation.

It is a natural part of the LOA that we tend to see more of what we look for in our lives. Even when it comes to the mundane things in life, patterns due to the LOA will tend to manifest and emerge when we are focusing on the good in our lives. Many people notice, for example, that once they pick out a car to buy, they will then see that particular model of car and/or color of car on the road with increased frequency. This emerging pattern is due to the LOA bringing you more of what you focus your attention upon; it is not a coincidence.

The point of the gratitude journals or gratitude lists is not just to have a long list of things you are thankful for. The exercise enhances your recognition of positive things. The goal is to become more present and receptive to all the good things that happen. So many good things take place every day that often go unrecognized people because they are focusing on what they want and don't have instead. However, even the smallest things that happen to you every day that are good should be acknowledged and appreciated.

You will find that if you get into a pattern in which you are constantly focusing on the positive elements in your life, eventually it will be easier for you to see what is going well for you. The pattern in your mind will shift to seeing more of the positives and less of the negatives. This type of switch is what we want to achieve in order to cultivate more positive energies and emotions. When you begin to take actions based on your desires and intents, you may find that things might not go exactly as you planned.

A newfound feeling of appreciation is also extremely useful in this situation as well. It is important to shift your thinking to seeing the good in situations. For example, let's say you are looking to make money online. You are following the steps in the LOA and consequently thinking about and visualizing success in the endeavor. You then take action and set up a website and place your products on this website seeking to make money to cover your bills and expenses.

Now, let's say you make no money the first month. As you are following the LOA, you take this development in stride and make some major modifications to this website. You remind yourself that part of the LOA is to proceed with a happy attitude and a smile on your face. You put your energies into visualizing making money and taking more positive actions with your business.

However, perhaps you also make no money on the website the next month. At this point, you have invested a considerable amount of time and money. You have bills hanging over your head that you need to pay, and fear starts to kick in. You start to worry that this venture might be a downhill battle.

At this point, it's a great time to utilize the power of appreciation and contemplate of what you are grateful for. The trick is to keep your thoughts and emotions focused on the positive aspects of the situation. At first it may be difficult for you to come up with any reasons or thoughts about what is good about losing time and money on a website that is potentially worthless. However, if you have been building up your strength and ability to recognize in your life what you are grateful for, it will be easier to see the good and positive outcomes of the situation. Remember, the more you practice feeling appreciation for everything you can, the more strengthened your abilities will be.

Practicing appreciation and contemplating gratitude are like practicing a sport or activity. Upon increased practice, you will become better and more flexible. Just as you would work out your muscles at the gym to make them stronger, consider that exercising feeling gratitude and thankfulness will also make it easier for you to consider stronger and better thoughts and feelings of appreciation. Like learning any skill or like learning to ride a bicycle, there may be times you fall off balance and need to recenter yourself. This is all part of the learning process. In this particular situation, you may be able to think of a variety of items to feel strongly thankful for relating to your web business. Even if it is not making money on the surface, there is plenty to potentially feel grateful for.

For example, your list of appreciations may include:

- I have now learned how to build a website on my own; this skill could come in handy down the road,
- In putting together this website, I worked closely with my children, who contributed ideas. This activity brought us closer together as family.
- I have more confidence in my computer skills after this experience.

The ability to turn thoughts that may be negative and doubtful at one point in your life into thoughts and feelings that now emanate harmony, balance, and happiness is a crucial skill to learn and cultivate.

FEEL THE POWERFUL EMOTION OF GRATITUDE

It is important to remember when making your list to *feel* the emotion of gratefulness while writing down your thoughts. It is your emotional intensity that will bring the most power and intensity into these positive signals you are putting out to the universe. When you write down each thing you are grateful for, remember to take a minute to feel the emotions connected with your appreciation.

Take some time out to breathe, shut your eyes, and consider how much happiness the items on your list bring into your life. You might even begin to feel your eyes well up with tears as you begin to truly understand how lucky you are for what you have. The more emotional you get, the more you will harness the powers of the LOA.

Also, throughout the day, pay attention to the good things that happen to you. Even small things that make you happy should qualify as items you pay more attention to and draw your focus toward. Remember these things and make a mental note to include them into your gratitude list. Maybe someone gives you a compliment at work, or you effortlessly get through a task during your day. Even if these things are small, they are not inconsequential because they are items that bring you positive energy and good vibrations. Perhaps you see an exceptionally cute dog running in the park or an exotic-looking bird while you are taking a walk. Take some time to appreciate the beauty of what you see around you. Think about how lucky you are to live in a world where you can freely experience viewing such marvels of nature. This is the positive energy you want to manifest more of in your life.

Contemplating what you are grateful for in your life will always rebalance your emotions and bring you back to your center. If you ever feel as though the LOA isn't working, or you get frustrated with the path you are on in life, you can always come back to making lists or just thinking about what you are grateful for to get back on track.

As long as you are living, there will always be something to be grateful for. Contemplating and feeling appreciative thoughts is always a tool that you have at your disposal to reactivate your positive energies. You always have the power to reach for a better and more uplifting thought. These ideas will always get your energies flowing in the right direction and assist you in beginning to manifest your desires.

6

You Are Your Own Creator

You are your own creator. This statement is one of the key principles to remember when utilizing the LOA to bring about positive results in your life. Another way to state this important phrase is simply: you create your own life. What this means specifically is that you have the power and potential to manifest the results you need at any given time.

The key to effectively using the LOA is to first understand that you have this capability, and then to use this newfound knowledge to direct your life in the way in which you want it to go. Once you realize that you are the sole creator of your life, you will start to realize that you have inner strengths and control over your life in a way in which you previously might have never thought possible. As you begin to realize that you create your own life, you will also release the tendency to ever feel as though you are a victim. In contrast to feeling weak or out of control, you will actually begin to feel more and more empowered to make positive choices in your life. You will find that when you think or act like a victim, more experiences come into your life that make you feel victimized. Alternatively, when you think and act as a powerful and dynamic person who makes good things happen, you will see good enter into your experience in a steady and rapid fashion.

As you change your thinking, you will become accustomed to guiding events and situations into happening. You will also start to experience what it is like to achieve the results you want and know that your thinking and actions caused these events and situations to manifest. This feeling is very empowering and life altering, to say the least.

In order to get the LOA to truly work to your benefit, it is essential to realize that you always direct your own life. This process occurs whether you consciously intend to direct the flow of what happens or not. Try to assimilate and fully understand this key concept. When you are consciously directing the flow of your life through your thinking and actions, the LOA works to bring about your goals.

Similarly, when you are not consciously directing your thoughts and actions, the LOA is still working in your life to produce results and reflecting your inner thoughts and outward actions. The LOA works 24 hours a day and 365 days a year, so even if you aren't trying to control it, you are still manifesting.

Once you start consciously directing the flow of your life, you eventually will learn how to effectively bring about the results that you want and avoid accidentally attracting what you do not want. We discussed this earlier in this book in Step Two: Knowing What You Do Not Want. This step is essential to understanding that you are your own creator and are thereby directing and controlling what you do indeed want into your life.

Your thoughts and actions are sacred. You need to not only monitor them closely, but also constantly work to guide them in the best direction possible.

CHOOSING YOUR FRIENDS AND ASSOCIATES

If you are serious about bringing about positive results in your life, you will need to leave behind situations and people that will not serve you in your new direction. Have you ever heard the advice that the associates that you seek out should be more successful than you? For example, Warren Buffet, who is one of the richest and most respected people in the world, has said, "It's better to hang out with people better than you...Pick out associates whose behavior is better than yours, and you'll drift in that direction." Indeed, this is a very important rule to consider. If you are spending your time with people who achieve less than you do, you may be bringing yourself down, so to speak, by sharing their thoughts, words, and conversations.

When reading this idea, many people will automatically think, *So I should drop my lifelong friends and relationships just because these people have less money and success than I do?* The truth of the matter is that during the time period in which you are developing your ability to use the LOA and bring about positive results in your life, yes, dropping these relationships is rather essential. In Chapter 4, we discussed re-evaluating your relationships, but it is important now to delve into this subject a bit deeper and explain why your relationships are so important when you are focusing on becoming a more active creator of your own life.

Take some time and carefully analyze the people you are spending most of your time with. Are these people frequently critical toward you? Do you ever feel as though they are judging you? Do you feel depressed and disheartened after speaking with them? If you can answer yes to any of these questions, you can safely conclude that these are not people you should be spending much time with.

Unsupportive and critical people can actually work against your progress with the LOA. It fact, it is truly important to spend the majority of your time with people who share similar goals and dreams. As we discussed in a previous chapter, we must always be "Changing Negative Images into Positive Ones." This thought holds true even when it comes to the images that result from spending time with people who are negative influences. However, when you are distracted by being in someone's presence, it can sometimes be difficult, if not impossible, to constantly be changing all the negative images that come into your mind and reframing them to positive visualizations. As hard as you may try, you will find it will be difficult to keep this up for long.

Have you ever been around someone negative and felt afterward as though they had literally drained you of all of your energy? This isn't just your imagination. Negative people have the power and capability to override our own natural thoughts and inclinations. With this said, however, it does not mean we should never talk to these people again. Obviously, if you have close friendships that you have developed over the course of your life, you need not abandon them. One suggestion would be to simply tell your friends of family members that you will be "going underground" for a period of time. Perhaps you can tell them that you are going to spend an extended period of time focusing on developing yourself, or your work. You can even tell them you are spending some time alone to "find yourself." The point is that you need some time away from these relationships.

As cliché as this statement sounds, the following point is true. If these people are truly your friends, they will understand and respect the fact that you need some time to yourself. It does not need to be something they take personally. Additionally, if these people are truly your friends, they would and should want what is best for you. In this case, what is best for you may be to avoid them, but you do not need to tell them that fact in such blunt terms.

The second point of contention people often have with the concept of controlling whom to spend time with is that they may feel that only spending time with those more successful than themselves will make them into some sort of friendship "gold digger." However, this idea is somewhat of a misinterpretation. This concept of spending time with those who are more successful than you is not intended to make you an obsequious person. We don't need to solely try to make friends just based on their wealth. Instead, the idea is to make friends and connections and spend your time with people you admire and who inspire you. Obviously there are many other things you can also respect and admire in people other than wealth. What you most want to do is spend time with others who have achieved something that you want to cultivate in your own life. This may be happiness, simplicity, education, money, career, relationships, etc.

Two crucial parts of the LOA are controlling our thoughts and controlling our actions. The people we spend time with are responsible in part for both our thoughts and our actions. It is important to monitor this activity and make sure it is in harmony with the results we want to see manifested in our lives. Thus, it is up to you to create your own life and achieve your own goals with the LOA. Part of this process is to take a good, long, and serious look at your own life. Spend some time to determine what it is that you can or should do differently. That process can help you bring about whatever it is that you want to achieve or receive.

By now you should realize that if you do not believe that you can achieve results, you will end up being absolutely correct. With this realization in mind, you should set out to examine your own life with fresh, new eyes. Life is full of challenges and obstacles. What separates people that get what they want out of life from those people who do not is their response to challenges. For example, if you are the kind of person that gives up easily or always experiences negative thoughts and/or emotions when confronted with a challenge, then it is unlikely that you will ever get everything you want out of life or that you will be able to use the LOA to its utmost potential.

FACING SETBACKS

How you address a setback, especially a major one, can play a large part in defining how your life unfolds. The examples are virtually endless. Losing one's job is an extremely traumatic event for most people. However, as we know, there are also countless stories of people who went on to get better jobs. One of the most important things you can learn to do is carefully tackle whatever comes into your life and ignore outward experiences and labeling situations as "negative."

Imagine for a moment that if you were fired from your job, you simply said, "Well, that's it, that is the best job I will ever get. I can't possibly do any better than that job, and I will never make that amount of money again." Guess what? You are instantly correct. By limiting your thinking, you have effectively attracted an outcome to yourself. That outcome will be that you are likely to not even try and get a better or higher-paying job because you have already limited your view of the universe. Again, you are your own creator. See how clearly this works?

While losing a job can be tough, if you believe in the power of your own thoughts and the LOA, you can use the experience of losing your job as an opportunity to improve your life. If you believe that losing your job is likely to be a positive event in the long term, the odds that it will turn out to be a positive event, of course, greatly increase.

Your thoughts create your reality. By seeing that job loss as an actual opportunity, you are taking an important step. The step you are taking is to realize that you are your own creator and acting upon this knowledge. Once you have taken that step, you can head out with confidence and seek a better job. Use your thoughts and actions to manifest one that pays more and that you like more.

You may even know someone who lost their job went on to start their own company, and became extremely successful In the case of this common example, when this person lost his job, he did not believe that it was "all over." Further, this belief wasn't just something he momentarily told himself to cheer up because this positivity was something truly felt at his core. Instead, he believed in himself and his potential, and he moved forward expecting something great to happen. He believed that he would find a way, and he did.

Many successful entrepreneurs believe that they are the creators of their own lives. As a result, countless success stories have been created. These people sometimes took the hard knock that life delivered, and set about controlling their thoughts, making their thoughts positive, and began building something new and prosperous.

For example: 5,127. That is the actual number of prototypes that James Dyson, of the Dyson vacuum cleaner fame, went through before settling on a design that he was satisfied with. It took Dyson many years to perfect his concept, and he and his wife lived on her modest salary as an art teacher while he worked on his invention.

Today, Dyson's personal worth is $2 billion. It is safe to say that he created an empire in the process. There were 5,127 opportunities for Dyson to say, "This will never work, and I have been doing this forever. I should just give up." The lesson here should be obvious in that Dyson's thoughts later shaped his reality. He believed with persistence that most people would have difficulty mustering. He steadfastly believed that he was onto something. That belief was his North Star, if you will, guiding him through the years. Finally the day came when his company took off. Most people would have given up. But buried in this story is a vitally important component that many would overlook, and that is Dyson's wife.

Deirdre Dyson worked for years as an art teacher while her husband pursued his dream of reshaping the vacuum cleaner industry. Her dedication to the idea that her husband was "on to something" was deeper than it might initially seem. Several arrogant manufacturers told Dyson that if there were a better way to build a vacuum cleaner, they would have done it. So James Dyson's wife Deirdre not only supported her husband's dream and quest to build the best vacuum the world had ever seen, she even did so after having executives at vacuum cleaner companies tell James that he didn't have "anything."

Deirdre Dyson is an excellent example of the importance of surrounding oneself with the right kinds of people. James Dyson managed to attract someone into his life who was capable of sharing his vision. It may very well be that with a less supportive spouse, Dyson may have been forced to go down a different path long before success arrived. Deirdre Dyson underscores the value of having the right people around you during your own personal quest.

Whom you choose to have in your life on a daily basis is obviously critical to your own success. Many of us are quick to dismiss this factor, even though it is so important. As human beings, by our very nature, we are social animals. Being with other people is healthy and natural, so we can't really exclude ourselves from the world completely for too long. However, if there are people around you that are preventing you from feeling positive or that you find are making you limit your perception of yourself and what you are capable of, you need to avoid them.

By allowing James to pursue what would someday become the Dyson empire, Deirdre Dyson was making a statement to him every day that she believed in him and what he was doing. Good spouses, good friends, a supportive family—they're going to believe in you and your quest.

Consider the following idea in terms of relationships. If your spouse leaves you, and your first thought is, *Well, that is it! I will never find anyone else again. No one will love me like he or she did. It's all downhill from here,* what do you think the odds will be that those words will become reality? Most of us know someone who went through a bad break up and never truly recovered. As a result, he never "aimed too high" and ended up settling. Often, this person settled for being treated poorly.

However, most of us have also seen the flip side of the story as well. It is common that after a relationship breaks up, someone who is a better fit comes along for both individuals. Much of this relationship success stems from how that person approached the situation. What he believed to be true affected the events that occurred next. His beliefs shaped his reality and helped shaped his fate. A broken-hearted person who quickly picks himself up and says, "I am a great, wonderful, and lovable person, and I will find someone who is the right fit for me. I will find someone who loves me more than my misguided ex did. I will be happier with that person than I have ever been before." Who has a better chance of being happy the person who knows it is all over or the person who believes that brighter days, full of even more love, are ahead of them?

Sometimes even the most unlikely event can have a positive overall impact on your life. For example, take someone who went through a very rough financial time and had his car repossessed. This person could very easily use the LOA on this "setback" to manifest a series of new and positive changes. As a result of losing his car, this person may have had no choice but to start walking and biking much more than he did when he had a car. He might think, *Something good will come out of this, it always does.* As a result of keeping his optimism and faith that positive forces were guiding him, good things will continue to occur.

After a few months, suppose this individual lost the fifty pounds that he had struggled to lose but never could. Perhaps he slowly became more fit and eventually began to not even miss the car. Over time he noticed that carrying his groceries home, for example, helped him lose the weight and keep it off and build muscle mass. Physically feeling better, his outlook and attitude changed. He actually found that he wanted to work out and began getting in even better shape. While at the gym, he found the woman he would eventually marry. Now, keep in mind that he would never have met this woman had he not had his car repossessed. This belief that something good would come out of a seemingly negative situation literally changed his life.

REFRAMING YOUR MIND

You are the one who decides what is and is not possible for your own life. There may be some aspects of life that we cannot control absolutely; however, thoughts do not fall into this category. Your thoughts are remarkably precious because they are the only thing that you can truly exercise absolute domain over. What you can potentially control completely on a minute-to-minute basis are your own mind and your own thoughts. The important thing is to learn to fill your life with joy and fulfillment and to guide your mental imagery toward your goals.

Eventually, as you progress in using the LOA, you will find that it becomes easier and easier to guide your thoughts into ones that benefit your life. When you first begin, you may find it challenging, but you will soon find that there are small changes and techniques that you can utilize in day-to-day life that will keep you on the right track. For example, most people dread the experience of facing a big stack of bills to pay. They set the bills aside and then pay them at the last minute, feeling aggravated and hassled. As you learn to become the creator of your own life and guide your life in a positive direction, even paying a stack of bills can be a joyous experience.

As you look at each bill, think of all the wonderful things that it represents to you. A utility bill, for example, may remind you how lucky you are to have electricity and heat. Take a minute and contemplate all the good that power brings into your life via your computer, your lights, your refrigerator, etc. If you are paying your rent or mortgage, think about how lucky you are to have shelter and a roof over your head, and how much you enjoy the space you live in. More importantly, use the exercise of paying your bills to guide you toward what you *do* want. In this particular situation, it is likely you want to pay off your bills completely and achieve the goal of being debt free.

While you are going through the process of paying the bills, visualize the day when you pay off your bills—what it will look like and how you will feel. As you look at the bill, think about how good it will feel as you go through the process of paying more and more each month and achieving the goal of erasing your debts completely.

The main idea of all of this is to practice reframing your thoughts so that even the most mundane activity now represents happiness to you and progress toward your goals. To continue with bills as an example, one exercise you can practice is to take a large bill and some whiteout. Erase the total amount that you owe on the bill with the whiteout and type a big zero over the amount that was previously listed. Place this new bill that indicates you owe nothing somewhere where you will frequently see it. For example, place it on your night-stand. Every night before you go to bed, look at this new bill announcing that you owe nothing. Think about how good it feels to have this bill paid off. Contemplate what you might do with this money instead. Drift off to sleep knowing that your bill is paid off, and spend the night having pleasant dreams.

Much of the universe is outside of your immediate control. A distant star going supernova is not only beyond your control, but you are also unlikely to even know it has occurred. Focus on your own thoughts. Remember, your thoughts create your universe. As a result, they are the most important component of attracting what you want into your own life.

7

Step Two: Know What You Do Not Want

It is almost as important to decide what you do *not* want as it is to decide what you do want. You may be wondering why you should focus on the negative, the things that you do not want, when your ultimate goal is to know what you do want. The reason is that knowing what you do not want will make figuring out what you do want a lot easier. During this step, many people realize that what they think they want is actually something that they do not want.

Our lives are oftentimes intertwined with others. What someone else wants (like a spouse for example) may not be what you want. In fact, you may come to realize that you do not want what your spouse wants at all.

What you think you want will be affected by things that are not actually part of your future vision. For example, you may think that you want to own a certain car, but perhaps that is part of a picture in your head from someone else's dream. So as you look at the complete picture of your future in the way that you want it to look, make sure that all of the components are things that you are emotionally connected to getting, things that you feel an affinity for, things that draw you to them and move you toward getting them. You are the only person who has control over what comes into your life, so it is important that you do not let others influence your vision. Make sure your vision works for you. If part of that picture does not work, acknowledge it and get rid of the parts that do not fit.

The purpose of figuring out what you do not want is to get it over with and put it behind you. Once you figure out what you do not want, you can think about it and then leave it and walk away. The importance of this is so that you no longer think about what you do not want. This chapter is supposed to help you switch your focus and make your transition easier from the negative (what you do not want) to the positive (what you do want). It's that simple.

An example of this concept in your every day life might be when you sort through your mail. What is that you do not want to see in your mail? Bills. You already know that you do not want to receive bills, so why focus on it? Instead, what you want to do is focus on what you do want to see in your mail. Maybe you want to receive a card from a loved one. Maybe you want to see a refund check. Perhaps you want to see an invitation to a fantastic event. Do you see where we are going with this? Your goal is to approach all angles of your life this way.

A part of your life that may not align itself with your new goals could be a relationship that is not appropriate for you. As we said before, as part of using the LOA, you should evaluate the people around you and ask yourself if they contribute positively to your well-being. For example, if you are in an intimate relationship with someone who abuses you, puts you down, or does not respect you, it will be very difficult for you to attract good experiences into your life with this person in it. If you have a friend that is not supportive and questions your goals or aspirations, you must question his friendship. All of the people you have relationships with, whether a significant other, family member, friend, or colleague, should be supportive of you and your goals and respect you for who you are. So evaluating your relationships is an important part of the LOA process. If an intimate relationship, friendship, or acquaintanceship is going to prevent you from attracting positive experiences into your life, then it is one you do not want.

Another part of your life that might not mesh with your goals could be living in an area that is not appropriate for you. Different locations mean different opportunities, whether you want to find your soul mate, start a business, send your kids to good schools, or lead a different lifestyle. You must ask yourself if where you are right now is going to allow you to reach all of your goals. If not, you may want to explore different towns, cities, or countries to find the perfect fit for you.

Maybe you have a job that you do not like. Perhaps you do not know what you want to do. This is the case for many people, and, at this stage of the LOA process, it is perfectly normal to not know exactly what you want. Perhaps you know that you are not happy with your current job but you want to explore other options. In this case, your current job is what you do not want.

Are you satisfied with the physical structure you are living in? Maybe you live in an apartment that you are growing out of. You may have been accumulating things and you need a bigger place. Or perhaps you live in a house, but you have a baby on the way and need an extra bedroom. Maybe you are not sure whether you want to rent or own, or you do not know exactly how much space you need or where you should live. All you know is that where you are living right now is causing you stress and you do not want to live there.

This next example of figuring out what you do not want consists of a broader example of the mail example previously mentioned. Many people are in debt. They have spent more than they can afford by purchasing houses, cars, and vacations. These items may make them happy in the short term, but their focus in the long term is all the debt they are accumulating. Focusing and worrying about debt is only going to dig you deeper into the hole. The important thing to do in this situation is to acknowledge that debt is something you do not want and to take action from this point on and in the future.

You must decide on exactly what you do not want. If you are going back and forth about whether or not you want something, then maybe you need to decide that it is right for you, with small changes instead. To go back to the relationship example, suppose you have a boyfriend and there are some qualities that you do not like about him. We are not saying you should sever the relationship. Rather, we are asking you to decide whether you want him in your life or not. If you decide you do want him in your life, then maybe there are specific qualities you need to talk about with him. Perhaps you want to stay in the relationship, but positive changes need to occur.

We are well aware that life is not black and white. It is not easy to say either stay or go, keep or throw away, but when looking at your life overall, there should be clear goals, and this step should help you find out what your goals and aspirations are. When you are planning and envisioning your future, you need to eliminate from that vision what you do not want. Focusing on what you do not want and worrying about having what you do not truly desire is only going to contribute more and more to what you do not want.

Now we have explained how important it is to know what you do not want. It is important to figure this step out and then, as you continue on with the steps of the LOA, you must try to forget about what you do not want. As soon as you move forward to Step Three, you'll want to forget what you do not want and start focusing on what you do want. Putting time and energy into what you do not want will not get you anywhere, so it is very important to eliminate these details in your mind so that you can move forward with the LOA and the steps we are outlining in this book. This is going to lead us into the next step. Step Three of this miracle process is "Know What You Do Want."

8

Step Three: Know What You Do Want

Knowing what you want is very important and you must be as clear as you possibly can in this step. You must shift your focus from what you do not want (what you already determined in the last chapter) to exactly what your vision is. Do you want better health? Do you want a better relationship? Do you want a better job? Do you want to become wealthy? Whatever it is, you need to be very clear on this step. You do not want to focus your attention on what it is that you do not want. Now is the time to get rid of those thoughts. You have already banished those things from your mind. In Step Two, you discovered what you do not want. Now, in Step Three, it's time to shift your attention to exactly what it is that you do want.

This is the exciting part! We really want you to get excited about using the LOA to attract new and better things into your life. This step will probably take you more time to master out than Step Two. There are so many aspects of our lives that influence us and we will outline some of the major ones in this chapter and the ones that follow. You have to figure out what you want and what will influence you the most in achieving a more positive life. Get excited about this step because you are about to see all the great things that you will soon have in your life.

The LOA states that you are basically a magnet, attracting the images that are inside your head. Whatever you are conceiving, you can also achieve, if you focus strongly enough. This is a very important step in the LOA process. You must be very clear about what you want.

It is important for you to take your time during this step. The few minutes it takes you to read through this step are not nearly enough for you to fully envision what you want to attract into your life. So go ahead and take an hour or even a few days to really think about what you want. We suggest you keep a notebook to write down ideas as you read this chapter; however, you will want to do a lot more than just write ideas down.

Your goal should be to decide once and for all what you want and write it down. The list can be long or short, but we do suggest that you make it as detailed as possible. You can divide your journal into different chapters of your life and dedicate a few pages to each chapter. Below we have outlined some key chapters that you may want to make your own. We also ask that once you decide on a specific list of chapter of your life, you list them in order of importance, starting with the most important. The list below is just an example:

1. Abundance
2. Happiness
3. Health
4. Wealth
5. Relationships
6. Stress Relief
7. Success
8. Career
9. Things
10. Lifestyle

In this chapter and the ones following, we will take the above ten items and go into more detail about each. We believe that the majority of our readers will benefit from all ten of these items and will want to use the LOA to improve each of them. If you think of a category that we have left out, by all means make it part of your LOA process. The goal here is for you to figure what you want to ask for from the universe using the LOA.

Remember the importance of visualization when going over each of these categories. If the visualization does not come to you at first, we encourage you to write details down in your notebook. While you are thinking about what you want, paint a very vivid picture of it in your mind and/or write it down on paper. If you want a house, then imagine all the tiny details about the outside and inside of the house. Ask yourself what you want the house to look like, smell like, sound like, and feel like. If you want to make a career change, then imagine yourself in the job that would be ideal for you. Imagine yourself working at this new career. Picture all the details about how this new job makes you feel. Whatever it is that you want, picture it and envision yourself having it.

WHAT CAN YOU ATTRACT WITH THE LAW OF ATTRACTION?

The beautiful thing about the LOA is that you can attract ANYTHING! That's right—you can attract health, wealth, happiness, love, material items, a better career, clarity, a stress-free life—the list is truly endless. What you want in your life is completely up to you. Only you are aware of what you want and what will make you happy and what will allow you to lead an abundant life. Whether you want material items or an abundance of positive energy, the choice is yours and you should take only your thoughts and feelings into account. When thinking about what would add to your life, it is important to think only of yourself. This is a time to be selfish and not consider anyone else's wants or needs. Only you are in control of you. And only you have the power of knowing what you truly want out of life.

Not only do you need to know what you want, you need to know exactly what it is that you want to get out of the LOA. You will need to dig deep during this step and really evaluate what you want to attract into your life. You will need to elaborate and focus on this particular step as much as possible, with as much detail as possible, for whatever it is that you are asking for.

Why do you want the things you are asking for? Will they bring you enjoyment, fulfillment, motivation, love, etc.? Make sure the outcome of attracting this particular thing will also be what you want. Try to think of things that will enhance your life and empower you to be the best you can be. It is important for you to live up to your potential, which is limitless. Remember, in order to reach your true potential with the LOA, you have to know exactly what you want and what will enhance your life and empower you.

When going over each of these categories, you must look inside yourself. You must find out what you truly want. This is a time to explore your inner wants and needs. For some, this may be difficult to do because you may have spent your lifetime looking for what other people want, as opposed to what you want. To use the LOA effectively, you must not think about what other people want. The LOA involves only you and improving your life. Again, take your time with this step. Explore all your chances, opportunities, and possibilities. Along the way, continue asking yourself what would make you happy. What would enhance your life? What would improve your life? What would change your life? You must be able to honestly answer these questions and feel good about the answers you come up with. When asking yourself what you want, you should always be able to say "*I want this!*"

9
Abundance

Expect your every need to be met. Expect the answer to every problem, expect abundance on every level.

—Eileen Caddy

What is abundance? It is an oversupply of something. Abundance is wealth and success and anything else you could possibly want. Abundance is fullness and the sense of feeling complete. It is what we all strive for in life. Being abundant means we are satisfied with all aspects of our lives. It means different things to everyone. One person may feel abundant only when they are happy and healthy. Another person may only feel abundant when they have three cars and a big house. We are all different and we all want different things in our life, but we can all attract abundance using the LOA.

We are operating on two assumptions: that abundance is something you want the universe to give to you, and that everyone wants abundance in their lives. Abundance is a positive thing, and is what makes us feel satisfied and fulfilled. As you are now figuring out what you want to attract, we want you to see the importance of abundance and realize that you can and will feel abundant with the LOA. From experience, we can tell you that the feeling of satisfaction with what you have is unlike any other feeling in the world. There is a sense of calmness and clarity when abundance is achieved. However, when you achieve abundance, it does not mean that you are finished setting goals and asking to attract more from the universe. It just means that you are happy with what you have received and if you received nothing else, you would still feel abundant.

Achieving abundance with the LOA is a process that takes time and has steps you will need to follow. Once you have decided that you want abundance, you will be ready to move on to the next step of the book and that is to ask the universe for abundance. When trying to achieve abundance, we suggest you use this book as a guide in helping you along in the process. The more you incorporate the steps we outline in this book, the more you will understand it and wonderful things will start to manifest in your life.

Below is a metaphoric exercise that we suggest incorporating into your life. The metaphor represents abundance. By reading this metaphor every day, you will create positive energy for the universe and you will help create abundance in your life.

I am a small plant—a plant that has the appropriate amount of nutrients, water and fertilizer to grow into a larger plant. As I see myself grow, I notice my leaves are very bright green. They face upward toward the sun, absorbing the sun's energy, taking that energy in, using that energy to grow and become much larger. The soil feeds the roots of a small tree now. As I continue to grow and reach higher and higher, I am expanding my possibilities. I absorb the sunlight. I absorb the warm beautiful sunlight and I become stronger and stronger, bigger and bigger, spiritually developing. Reaching forward higher and higher, becoming more and more abundant and I am now imagining myself as a tree. I see that I am able to give back to the environment. I am able to provide shade, shade for the creatures around me, and protection. I am so relaxed as I continue to grow, to expand higher and higher, becoming a very beautiful tree. So very, very beautiful and I am a very special tree because I produce beautiful flowers, much like the lotus flower, for all to enjoy. I am abundance. I attract wealth. I attract happiness. I allow these energies to flow through me and I give back wealth in the form of my talent and the form of my abilities. I am now part of the cycle of giving and taking. Wealth and happiness flow through me. I am able to easily attract money because money flows through me. I give a portion of that money back to the universe and continue the cycle and continue to grow and continue to reach higher and higher. I am so very abundant now as I imagine myself as a very tall, very powerful tree with extensive roots. I am very strong and I will continue to grow in this manner. Growing higher and higher, reaching higher and higher, continuing to grow, continuing to grow spiritually, to grow financially, to grow emotionally, to grow creatively, and to grow in happiness. I will continue to grow in all of these ways. I *am* abundance.

This is a script has been shown to create abundance and confidence in people. By reading this script, you are telling the universe that you want abundance in your life. You want to grow and eventually give back to the world around you.

You can create abundance in your life using the LOA in so many different ways. A great way to create abundance in your life is starting with your thoughts and emotions. You can start by just feeling abundant. Focus on the areas of your life that you already feel abundant in, or are thankful for in some capacity. Creating emotions of abundance has a powerful effect. You cannot create these emotions if they do not exist; you have to feel the abundant emotions that are already within you. You have abundant feelings; you just have to tap into them. Creating feelings of abundance will create powerful vibrations for the universe. You can also think abundantly. Look at your life and see the wonderful things you already have. When you think about the areas of your life that help you feel abundant, this creates positive vibrations and positive energy. The universe will pay attention to your abundant thoughts and reward you with more abundance. Abundance is powerful.

10

Happiness

But what is happiness except the simple harmony between a
man and the life he leads?

—Albert Camus

What is life without happiness? How many people can truly say
that they are happy? They may say that they are happy with some
aspects of their life, but that other aspects need improving. Your goal
with the LOA should be to create happiness in all aspects of your life.
When asked the question, "Are you happy?" your response can and
should always be, "yes."

Happiness is qualitatively different from abundance. You can be
blissfully happy and have very little. Happiness is a state of mind and
the more happiness you put out, the more you will get back. Happiness is also a feeling, a feeling that you are in control of. Happiness is
joy, pleasure, and empowerment. It has been proven that you can
improve your mood and your happiness with your thoughts (Erber &
Erber, 2000).

It can be helpful to think of happiness in two different ways, using
the visual representation of a pyramid. Imagine two different pyramids and then imagine that these two pyramids hold your emotions.
You have pyramid one and pyramid two. Pyramid one represents the
goal of achieving happiness because happiness is the small point at
the top of the pyramid. It can seem unattainable if you are at the base
of the pyramid, but it is the shining pinnacle of what you are working
toward. The base of pyramid two is happiness, because happiness is

69

what you need the most of and it supports all other emotions. As long as you have happiness you have a good and strong base.

Using the representation of the two pyramids, you can use the LOA with pyramid number one in order to reach happiness. It is at the very top of the pyramid one and you work on moving up, through all the other emotions, to reach happiness. Once you reach the top of pyramid one, you have then created pyramid two. Happiness increases exponentially and creates the base of all your feelings and emotions.

If happiness is what you want from the universe, you must do everything in your power to receive happiness into your life. The more happiness you put out into the universe, the more you will get back. We suggest that you do something every single day that increases your happiness. Whether it is for five minutes or five hours, anything that you can add to your life that produces internal happiness will benefit you. When you are happy, vibrations become alive and the universe pays attention to the positive energy you are giving off.

It has been shown that regular exercise can make you happier. It makes sense that with this book, you are performing mental exercises with the LOA to improve your life. It also makes sense that you would do physical exercises to improve your happiness. Exercise assists regulates hormones such as cortisol. Cortisol is a hormone that is released in your body and that helps you return to a more normal and relaxed state when you are stressed or anxious. Endorphins are also released when you exercise. Endorphins act as your body's natural way of relieving pain and make you feel better. When you exercise, your body is releasing energy and you can definitely feel that energy! The universe can sense the energy as well. Exercise is just one thing that can make you happier. The good news is that there are thousands of other things that can make you happier as well.

Another example of something that can make you happier is meditation or prayer (McGowan, 2005). Studies have shown that people who are spiritual are more likely to describe themselves as being very happy than people who do not consider themselves to be spiritual. According to an article in Time magazine, having friends has a lot to do with happiness, and having close relationships with friends and family directly contributes to our happiness.

We are not mandating that you go exercise or be spiritual; rather these are just examples that can help you explore what will make you happy. The important thing to do is to continually do things that make you happy because happiness gives off radiant energy and the more radiant energy you give off, the more you will receive. Also, happiness is contagious not only for you in your own life, but for others around you. Giving off happiness tells the universe to deliver more happiness back into your life. When you exude happiness to the people around you, they will subconsciously become inspired and start changing as well. Everyone wants to surround themselves with happy people, but by attaining happiness yourself, you improve their happiness without them realizing it and this in turn improves your relationship with them. As you can see, happiness is powerful; it is an integral part of our life and directly influences all parts of our life.

By now you have most likely decided that you want happiness in your life. We encourage you to continue exploring different things that make you happy in your life. If it is a change in attitude that makes you happy, then we encourage you to change your attitude. If volunteering your time makes you happy, then go for it! The important thing is that you are happy! Part of the LOA is incorporating the things that you want into your life. Again, if you want happiness in your life, in order to receive it from the universe you must do things that make you happy or promote happiness. The more often you have thoughts and feelings of pure happiness, the sooner the LOA will reward you with happiness.

An exercise to help you with this that you can do every day is to have a journal and write down things that make you happy. It can simply be something that made you smile that day, or maybe something that you are thankful for. The more often you can think or write down a happy thought or feeling, the better. We suggest you write at least one thing a day, but if you are able to write twenty, then go for it! For example, if you had a conversation with someone that made you happy, write that down in one or two sentences. If the weather was beautiful outside, write that down. If you helped someone or they helped you and that made you smile, write it down. After awhile, if you start getting the same feeling from thinking about the happy things that occurred during your day instead of writing it, then that is fine and maybe you don't have to write it down. Perhaps you can mentally try to think of five things every day that made you smile or made you happy. If five is too easy for you, you can think of more. The point is, the more happy thoughts you think about in one day, the more the happiness the universe is going to reward you with.

Another suggestion would be to create a gratitude journal. A gratitude journal is where you write down things that you are thankful for in your life. Writing down positive things you are thankful for will create positive vibrations for the universe. It will also help you with the process of the LOA. Focusing on the things you already have helps during the process. It is important to be grateful both before you receive what you want with the LOA and after you have received what you have been asking for. Being appreciative for good things in your life is going to contribute immensely to your happiness. Research has shown that happier people are those who greater appreciation in their lives in general (Tucker, 2007).

11

Health

Health is a state of complete physical, mental and social well-being, and not merely the absence of disease or infirmity.

—World Health Organization, 1948

Perhaps good health is the most important thing you wish to attract. If you or a loved one have ever had your life or health compromised in a serious way, you know how important it is. Whether you want to improve your health or maintain good health, you can do so with the LOA. Adopting a healthy lifestyle has many long-term benefits (Jackson, Tucker, & Herman, 2007).

Although your body may seem like a physical entity, it is also a creation of your thoughts. You are unlimited in your ability to heal. Your mind is in control of your body, your muscles, your ligaments, your tendons, your joints, your bones, your arteries, your veins, your organs, your hormones, and every cell in your body. In Step One of this book, you learned how to control your thoughts and emotions. This next step will prepare you to improve your health. Believe it or not, the same way you took control of your thoughts, you can take control of your health.

If a healthy body is what you are seeking with the LOA, incorporate visualization and imagine your mind healing the various parts of your body that need healing, all the way down to the cellular level. You are capable of healing yourself. We know it is hard to wrap your mind around, but yes, you can heal your body.

Below is a sample script that can help you improve your health. We encourage you to use it as an affirmation that you can make yourself feel better and attract better health into your life.

I imagine my body to be a glass cylinder standing upright. My body is a glass cylinder. Now I imagine that in through the top of my head there is a green, cleansing, soothing liquid pouring in, into the glass cylinder which is my body, in through the top of my head and as it pours in it begins to fill my body just like a glass. It is filling my body from the bottom up, so as the liquid pours in through my head it goes all the way down to my feet, warming my feet, relaxing my feet, soothing my feet. The warm, healing, cleansing liquid begins to move up now, up my legs, up to my knees, relaxing me as it fills up my body, moving up to my thighs now, relaxing my thighs completely, moving up to my pelvic area, to my abdominal area. Relaxing and soothing all of the muscles and all of the organs of my body as it rises slowly. Moving up now to my chest area, relaxing, cleansing, healing all of the organs in my chest area. Now I feel it pour down to my arms and starting with my finger tips, the warm, soothing liquid moves up to my hands and my wrists, my forearms, my elbows, all the way up my arms, all the way up to my shoulders. Now my entire body is full all the way up to my neck and it feels so good and relaxing and the healing, cleansing, relaxing liquid moves up to my face, relaxing my mouth, my cheeks, my nose, my ears, my eyes, my eyebrows, my forehead all the way up and now my body is completely full of the relaxing green liquid. This color has been chosen because green is the color of healing. Plants are green; plants are so full of energy. Green, for a long time, has been known as the color of healing. So I relax now as the green liquid begins to warm slightly and as it does, it activates all of the cells in my body, cleansing them, healing them. I think of this green liquid as a perfect antioxidant because it is now cleansing all of the cells in my body. I feel my body come into harmony now with itself and with its surroundings as I enjoy perfect and radiant health. The liquid warms a little more now and I relax even more deeply. I feel every cell in my body being energized and cleansed and healed and if there is any challenge in any part of my body, I feel that part being healed now, cleansed, purified. I feel the cells of that part of my body releasing any toxins where they will be properly dealt with by my body and eliminated by my body. I feel this process happening now. Every time I read this affirmation, I can choose to work on a particular part of my body, perhaps a muscle, perhaps an organ in my body. Perhaps I just want to work on general health and energy. Now is that time to work on that part of my body that I have chosen if I have chosen one. I feel an extra amount of warmth in that part of my body, the part that is now being cleansed and healed and receiving special attention. Perhaps there is more than one part. I now relax that part of my body and feel the warmth there. The green liquid is working extra hard to relax this part of my body and cleanse it. Cleansing my body naturally, I feel this process continuing long after I stop reading this script, cleansing, healing, repairing, and restoring that part of my body or these parts of my body, giving them that special attention until they are healed. Now I imagine that at the bottom of each of my feet the liquid is now draining out of my body and I can think of this process as an oil change of a vehicle. The oil goes into the engine, lubricates the engine, cleans the engine and then it needs to be changed. I am releasing the green liquid now, and I notice it is a little dirty. It has picked up a few toxins from my body and it is now releasing them out through the bottom of my feet so that the next time I perform this process, my body will already have been cleaned. Each time I repeat this process my body becomes cleaner and cleaner, more and more free of toxins. My body is almost empty now of the green liquid which has turned a slight brown color. It is a little dirty, but that is normal and natural because it has cleansed my body. All of the toxins are leaving my body now and now as the last few drops drain out, my body fills itself with natural energy. I can imagine this to be any color I want. I feel my body filling itself from every cell of my body with natural, vital energy allowing me to enjoy perfect and radiant health. I am developing healthy habits, eating things which are healthy for me, avoiding things which are unhealthy. Choosing exercise on a regular basis, keeping my mind healthy as well with positive thoughts, powerful, productive ideas, and taking care of my spiritual health. If I have faith, I find myself more interested in that faith because I take care of my spiritual health. Mind, body, and soul, in perfect harmony, in perfect balance, the way I was designed to operate. So I relax now and realize that everything is going to be just fine because day by day, I am becoming more and more healthy. The natural state of my body is a healthy state. My body is now instructed to be in perfect, perfect health. To be in perfect and radiant health.

If better health is what you seek, you can use the script and read it every day to improve your state of mind in relation to your health. Reading the script and relaxing as you do so will create positive energy. It is important to note that, when healing your body, it is imperative to think in terms of 'healing' and 'improving.' This adds positive energy to the healing process, whereas 'fighting' adds negative energy. Focus your attention on healing and positive energy will go to that area.

It has been scientifically proven that stress leads to health problems. An article in the *Journal of Personality and Social Psychology* found that there are significant relationships between stress and health problems such as influenza, headaches, backaches, sore throat, upset stomach; the list goes on and on. They also concluded that people with limited psychosocial support were more at risk for developing a sickness when their stress increased. By reducing this stress and healing the damage it has done, you can heal yourself with your mind (Delongis, 1988).

We want to point out the link between negative stress and your body's negative physiological response to the stress. When you become stressed, your immune system becomes taxed, making it weaker and more difficult for it to defend itself against sickness and disease. In this case, if you allow stress into your life, your body is more likely to develop a sickness such as a cold or flu. Allowing stress into your life is your indirect way of telling the universe that your body is prepared to fight off disease, but it is not. It is the exact opposite. Your body becomes weakened due to the stress.

You do not want this and you can prevent it! Just as you have already learned to control your thoughts, you can control your health. By refusing to allow stress into your life, you can keep your immune system strong and healthy. We understand that life happens and you cannot always control what happens to you, but you can control how you react to negative things. When you begin reacting in a healthy and positive way, the universe takes notice and you will realize that less negative things are occurring in your life. This applies to your health as well. You have to remain positive in order to heal yourself. By remaining positive, you are giving out energy that the universe pays attention to and will in return give back more health and radiance. Making things as easy as possible for yourself and not adding extra pressure or stress into your life is *your* responsibility and it will help you achieve perfect health with the LOA.

If perfect health is what you want from the LOA, then you must really think about what perfect health means to you. We are all different, so perfect health is a different concept to everyone and it is subjective. To one person, perfect health might be to rid their body of cancer. To another, it may mean feeling energized instead of fatigued. Perhaps you want to start drinking more water. Staying hydrated is very important to your health and it can lead to improvements in all areas of your life (Ritz & Berrut, 2008). Whether you want to lose weight, eliminate arthritis, manage your diabetes, control your blood pressure—whatever it is that will make you feel as though you are in harmony with your body—that is your definition of perfect health and you must keep this definition in mind when asking the universe for perfect health.

If you want better health, where exactly do you see yourself? Perhaps you want to improve your cholesterol and blood pressure levels. Maybe you have a specific workout goal such as losing weight. Do you see yourself running a marathon every year or being able to take a jog around the park every day? Envision it. Envision what it would be like to complete a marathon. How do you feel after knowing that you successfully completed 26.2 miles? How does it feel? Envision yourself winning a marathon, holding up a trophy, and waving to all the fans.

Your actions in relation to your health also affect what the universe will give to you. You have many actions in your life that directly contribute to your health. We have listed some of them below:

- Exercise
- Eating properly
- Not smoking
- Drinking in moderation

The opposites of the actions: not exercising, eating poorly, smoking, and drinking heavily all create negative vibrations. You do not want that! You want perfect health! Your actions must align with what you want. There is no easy way around this step. If being healthy is what you want, you must make the right decisions every single day.

12

Wealth

Wealth is the product of man's capacity to think.

—Ayn Rand

One of the biggest obstacles to overcome in regards to accumulating wealth is removing your focus away from your *lack* of money. This is what most people think about when they do not have the amount of money they want. They think, "How am I going to pay the bills? There is not enough money in my bank account." Or they say, "I want to buy that ring, but I cannot afford it." You must practice moving your focus away from your lack of money and start focusing on exactly how much you want; it is all about your mindset.

We will start with an example of exactly what it is we are referring to. Begin with the most common intention: you want to earn more money in your career. If you are still waiting for that raise that has not come, here is a suggestion. Write a fake check and fill it in with the exact amount you are looking for in your big pay raise. If you do not have a checkbook, simply create your own check on a blank piece of paper in the same fashion. The next step is to take this check with you and literally surround yourself with it. Hang it in a place where you will be able to see it several times a day, so it never leaves your train of thought. Whether you choose to hang this check in your cubicle, on your desk or even carry it in your pocket, make sure you take the time to stare at it several times a day. This will give you the feeling of what it would be like to already have that raise, and it will also provide you with the feeling that you already have what it takes within yourself to achieve this raise. You are staring at what it would look like and holding it, so you know what it would feel like to have it in your grasp; this is what we mean by surrounding yourself with it.

Do you want more money? How much money do you want? This all goes back to Step Two in the process of knowing what it is that you want. You need to be very clear about this step. For example, don't just say that you want more money—have a number in your mind. How much do you want in your bank account? Do you want fifty thousand dollars? Seventy five thousand dollars? Two hundred and fifty thousand? Take an exact number, and envision yourself already having that money. Imagine opening up a bank statement and seeing that number at the bottom of the page.

You want to ask for wealth. Not only do you want to ask to be wealthy, you want to ask for a specific dollar amount. Simply telling the universe that you want to be wealthy is not going to cut it. You must say to the universe that you want to attract wealth in the form of $_____. Go ahead and visualize the amount of money you want. Visualize what your bank statement would look like. Visualize it in your check book. Imagine the places you could go and the things you could buy. The key here is visualization. You are focusing on the money you will have and what you would do with the money in the present, acting as if you already had the money.

There are several ways you can incorporate wealth using the LOA, but if you think of one that works better for you that we fail to mention in this book, by all means, go for it! The goal is to attract wealth. One way of attracting wealth into your life is to decide on an amount of money you want in a specific time frame. Do you want to be worth $100 million by the time your retire? Do you want to make $100,000 over the next year? Do you want to accumulate $1 million by the age of thirty or forty? Do you work off of commission and you want a $10,000 payday?

All of these examples begin with the number *1,* and what you will want to do is take a $1 bill and add the number of zeroes to it with a permanent marker to create the goal amount you want. Put the bill where you will see it and think about it every day or several times a day. For example, tape it to your ceiling above your bed so that you will think about it every night before you fall asleep and every morning when you wake up. You can tape it to your bathroom mirror and think about it while you are brushing your teeth. You can keep it in your pocket or wallet and just take it out and look at it every day. No matter where you put the money, the important thing is that you look at it frequently and visualize your life with that amount of money. It is also important that you ask the universe to give you the money and just as important that you allow it to come to you. We will focus more on these two steps later in the book.

Another way to attract wealth into your life is to take an actual $100 and keep it in your wallet at all times. Whenever you see something you like for under $100, you'll want to mentally think about purchasing that item with the $100. The great thing about this method is that you can mentally spend hundreds or thousands of dollars in one day. You can browse the Internet and "spend" that $100 bill multiple times and feel like you are purchasing items you want. This will give you the sense of having wealth. Every time you mentally spend that $100, you are sending out positive energy to the universe, telling the universe that you want all these things. Believe us when we say the universe is paying attention. As long as you are giving off good positive vibrations, the universe will reward you in a positive way.

However, if you are mentally going through the process of spending the money but are secretly bummed out that you are not actually going to physically have these items, then you are putting out negative energy. It is true that you are not actually purchasing the items, but you could be, and you should be thinking that soon you will be able to purchase all these things.

It is important that you feel rich and abundant as often as possible in order to attract wealth successfully. Anything that you can do to aid your quest for wealth will help you attract wealth with the LOA.

You can also attract wealth by creating wealth boards. To do this, get a bulletin board, and when you see something you want in a magazine, cut the item out and tack it to the board. If you think of something you want to buy, write it down in detail on a piece of paper and tack it to the board. The possibilities are endless with a wealth board. You can cover every inch with things you want. We suggest you write down the amount of money you want to attract and put it on the board. You can even tack money itself to the board if you like.

Another method that is similar to the wealth board is to create a wealth box. You can put money in it. You can cut things out of magazines. You can put anything in it that represents wealth in your mind. You can add zeros to the amount on your monthly bank statement and put your bank statements in the box. Fill it with as many things as you can that represent wealth. If you have foreign money from international travel that you cannot use, go ahead and put that money in your wealth box. The more detailed you are about the things that you want that represent the wealth you will have, the more likely you are to attract them.

Also, make daytime affirmations about the wealth you wish to accumulate. Whether you read the affirmations out loud or to yourself, keep in mind that you also want to feel these statements as you read them. Creating positive feelings as a result of what you are reading will create powerful energy for the universe. Below is a sample of the script Steve uses in his Unlimited Wealth self-hypnosis recording that you may find helpful in your quest for wealth:

> I am unaffected by negativity and retain the ability to enjoy all of the warmth and joy that life has to offer. I am totally detached from negativity. I am open and receptive to wealth. I do not complain. I accept other people as they are and I do not expect them to change. I am patient, calm, and harmoniously centered at all times. I let go of all fear-based emotions such as blame, jealously, guilt, and possessiveness. These negative emotions are now a part of my past, and I open myself to receive all the good things life has to offer. I accept all good things into my life, especially wealth. I know that I am worthy of receiving all good things in my life including wealth. I allow myself to receive good things. I do not block good things from entering my life. I am worthy of receiving wealth into my life. I allow money to come to me. I allow money to come to me. I allow money to come to me. I now have a flow in my life, and money is actually attracted to me and I allow it to come to me. I do not stand in the way of money flowing toward me. I allow wealth to come to me. I know it is for me. And I know that I will use it for the greatest good. I allow wealth to come to me. I now realize that I have the ability to create in my life unlimited wealth. Unlimited wealth. My wealth will be without limits. I allow money to flow to me and it does. Wealth flows to me easily and effortlessly because I am now open and receptive to all good things. I keep my mind calm like water. I remain centered at all times. I am physically relaxed, emotionally calm, mentally focused, and spiritually aware and money flows to me. I now realize that I will have unlimited wealth. I will have all the wealth I desire and I let this happen easily and effortlessly. I am comfortable with wealth.

We have all heard the quote, "Money isn't everything." This is true, money is not everything, but it is a part of your life—for better or worse—and having money can make things a little easier for you. Having money allows you to go to places you want to go and see things you want to see and buy things you want to buy. Having money is a goal, and it is a good thing!

If you describe yourself as someone who worries about money, then you need to change your attitude to make the LOA work for you. Worrying is a negative emotion; negative emotions create negative energy. You want to change your attitude, along with your thoughts and emotions, to start thinking about money in a positive way. Focusing on what you *will have* rather than what you *do not have* is the best way to create positive vibrations for the universe and to make the LOA work for you.

We would like to give you a more specific example of someone who has used this method of surrounding yourself with all of this and found ultimate success. We are talking about the world-renowned actor Jim Carrey. He wanted to be an actor making a lot of money, and this is what he did about it. He wrote himself a check for $20 million and carried it around with him. He looked at it as often as possible. As we mentioned, this is a very effective way to reinforce an image in your head everyday. By looking at this check every morning, it was already making him feel like he had $20 million. Everyone knows how successful he has been.

Do everything in your ability with your thoughts, emotions, feelings, actions, and visualizations to tell the universe that you want to attract wealth. The examples we have given above are just that—examples. If vision boards are not something you will keep up with, then that is fine—they are just not the method for you. But hopefully we have sparked an interest in you that will encourage you to think of additional ways in which you can tell the universe you want to attract wealth. We hope you at least decide on an amount of money you want and surround yourself with that amount visually, mentally, and physically every single day.

13
Relationships

*"Don't settle for a relationship that won't let you be
yourself."*

—Oprah Winfrey

The category of relationships includes both love and friendship. It is natural for humans to develop relationships with others. Humans are intelligent, social, and nurturing beings who have an innate need to form bonds with others like us. Friendships with others are not always easily formed. It takes trust and support, but friendship is vitally important because it contributes to our overall well-being. Having close friendships or being in a close relationship can provide hope, happiness, and a positive outlook. Research has also shown that social relationships are significant correlatives and predictors of happiness (Holder & Coleman, 2009). In contrast, people without close friendships or relationships with others can feel like outcasts and feel discouraged. Having no or poor relationships with people can often lead to more negative behaviors such as overeating and substance abuse (DuPont, 1997).

Having relationships with people is important for all aspects of your life. Being in an intimate relationship with someone who loves and supports you will contribute to your feelings of love and well-being. Russell and Wells (1994) found that the strongest predictor of happiness in a marriage is the quality of marriage. Being in an intimate relationship with someone who disrespects you in any way or puts you down will have the opposite effect and can be highly detrimental to your well-being.

Using the LOA, your goal might be to find your soul mate, or perhaps you want to create new friendships with like-minded people. Whatever your purpose is regarding any relationship, you must figure out exactly what you want. If you want someone to confide in, imagine that person. If you want a boyfriend or girlfriend, imagine your ideal partner. If you want someone to spend time with on weekends and have fun with, imagine that person and the things you would do together. Remember, you have to know what you are looking for in order to ask for what you want.

So many people are looking for that special someone. If you are looking for a girlfriend, boyfriend, or your soul mate, you must realize that the LOA also applies to love. Love is a powerful force. Love involves your thoughts, feelings, and actions. It is an all-consuming energy that everyone deserves to experience. When love is involved, you must leave past relationships and transgressions at the door. Focusing on why past relationships did not work puts all of your energy toward negativity. Instead, we encourage you to focus your energy on your present and future.

Remember how we were talking about visualization earlier? Visualization plays an extremely important role in attracting a significant other. You must picture yourself meeting that special someone and having a great time. You should imagine what he or she looks like, what his interests and likes are, how he smiles, and what his laugh sounds like. You should imagine every detail, including the clothes he wears and the kind of job he has. Imagine your ideal date. You should also imagine how she will make you feel. She will bring out the best in you, making you a better person.

Let us move now to relationships. You more than likely already have a vision of the type of person you want to be with in your mind. What does this person look like? Do you already know this person? These are the questions you want to ask yourself, and more important, find an exact answer to. If it is at all possible, obtain a picture of this ideal person. Take this picture and hang it in your cubicle or on your wall and stare at it as much as possible. This is going to further amplify the image and what it will feel like when you are finally together. We have provided you with a few different examples but as you can see this process can work with literally anything you want!

A lot of people have an easy time imagining their perfect mate and asking the universe for this specific person. However, a lot of people have a hard time allowing that perfect person into their lives. You must be willing to open yourself up to allowing that perfect person into your life. If you suffer from fear of commitment, now is the time to work on overcoming this fear. Fearing commitment or fearing someone will leave or abandon you does not show the universe that you are allowing someone into your life. You must be willing to risk love to allow love into your life.

Receiving love is very similar to allowing love. When the universe tells you that you have found your perfect match, you should be thankful that the universe was listening. Continuing to focus on the positive energy of the relationship will help you fully receive this perfect mate so that you both can develop your relationship and give and receive love.

Perhaps you are already in a serious relationship, but you want to improve your relationship with this person. Acitelli, Kenny, and Weiner (2005) found that similarity and understanding in a partner's ideals leads to greater satisfaction in a relationship. They also found that when men show more understanding for their wives or girlfriends, discord decreases. The LOA can help you in this situation as well. Think about what would improve your relationship. It is important to remember when doing so that you can only change yourself and not your partner. If you want to improve communication with this person, you have to be more communicative. Picture the two of you involved in conversation and working on improving your relationship. Imagine how that would make you feel. Remove all negative emotions and do not think about the past. Focus on your bright future and your love for this person. Prisbell and Andersen (1980) found that being positive and feeling good are predictors of communication in relationships. Feeling good can lead to better communication.

Perhaps you want to be in a great relationship. What attributes are you looking for in another person? Do you want him to be kind, loyal, fun, wealthy, and attractive? Or maybe you want to be in a relationship with someone who is energetic, serious, active, and caring? Think about what is important to you and then picture it in the person you want to be with. Do you want to have children with this person? Do you want him to be motivated in his life as well? We already know that you want someone who is positive!

The truth of the matter is that it does not make any difference what you want. What you need to know is how to use this process of the LOA. You are learning how to use the six steps and how to use the extra tools that we are sharing with you to put everything together so that it works in synergy with the ultimate goal of bringing you everything that you ever wanted. Again, this is very important. Envision the

details of what you want. If you want a better relationship, what kind
of person do you want to be with? Know as many details as possible
about what it is that you are asking for. You must be clear about what
you want. This is what we are talking about when we say clear—you
have to know exactly everything about what you are asking for.

Relationships with friends are important to all of us. We all want to
attract quality relationships with people who share common interests
and who will be supportive. With friends, you are looking for a relationship that has value. Obviously, value means different things to different people. Qualities that you may seek out in a friend may be very
different than what other people seek out in friendship. It is usually
when this sense of value aligns and similar qualities are sought after
that a friendship is likely to form.

When using the LOA to attract friendship, you must first ask yourself what it is that you want in a friendship. What qualities must the
other person have? Do you care if they are male or female? Perhaps
you want someone to talk to, go out with, and participate in hobbies
together. In this case, you want someone who has similar interests as
you. Maybe you want her to be a good listener, honest, loyal, fun,
understanding, talkative, and have a sense of humor. The qualities you
seek will be important to you and it is important that you know what
you want in a friend so that you can use the LOA productively.

Friendships are an important part of our well-being. We look for
similarities in our friends of qualities that we also see in ourselves.
We often look for sincerity. Ralph Waldo Emerson once said, "A
friend is a person with whom I may be sincere." We want to be able to
talk with friends openly and honestly about what is going on in our
lives, and we want them to do the same with us. Perhaps you want a
few good friends in your life. Picture these people and the kinds of
relationship you want with them. Maybe you have good friends
already but you want to attract another friend that really makes you
laugh. You want to attract someone with a great sense of humor. Or
maybe you want someone who will listen to you and make herself
available to you at any time. Whether you are looking for many, a few
or one specific friend, decide on exactly what you want.

Visualize friendships in your mind. Imagine where you would go
and what you would do. Imagine what your friend would look like.
Imagine the conversation that would take place. Imagine enjoying
yourself in their company. Imagine them having a good time with you
as well. If you want more than just one friend, visualize spending time
with lots of friends. For example, picture a party where you are

friends with almost everyone and you are having a great time and enjoying yourself. Whatever it is that you want in relation to friendships, relationships and love, ask for it, picture it, allow it to happen, and then receive it.

Other relationships that are often very important are those with co-workers and superiors. How you interact with other people that you work with every day can have a dramatic impact on your life. Clydesdale (2009) found that workplace relations have a major impact on how people perform their jobs. As much as possible, surround yourself with positive people only. This is perhaps the most important rule of all the LOA principles. For us, surrounding ourselves with positive people is the most important rule there is. This is literally the beginning to finding a new life.

14

Relief from Stress

This art of resting the mind and the power of dismissing from it all care and worry is probably one of the secrets of energy in our great men.

—Captain J. A. Hadfield

Stress tends to contribute a lot of negativity to our lives. Stress can affect our health, our ability to think, our emotions, and our behaviors (Kotz, 2006). However, just as we have already learned that we can change the way we think, feel, and act, it follows that we also have the ability to manage our stress.

The most simplistic definition of stress is mental or physical tension. You probably are familiar with stress and how it makes you respond in your life. Stress can make us become irritable, irate or generally unable to react in calm ways. It is often the case that something happens in your environment that causes change, and it is this change that triggers stress. However, stress is something you do have control of in your life, and by using the LOA, you can receive relief from stress.

Stressful life experiences and the ways people cope with those stressful events have an impact on health and illness (Taylor, 1999, as cited in Taylor, Peplau & Sears, 2000). Stress can have a major impact in all of these areas and can also cause physical symptoms in our bodies. The following is a chart which illustrates how stress can affect each one of these areas:

Thoughts	Feelings	Actions	Physical Symptoms
• Inability to make decisions • Forgetfulness • Worry • Lack of focus • Loss of humor • Inability to see things for how they actually are • Loss of creativity	• Anxiety • Hopelessness • Anger • Frustration • Nervousness • Fear • Irritability • Sadness • Despair • Pessimism	• Criticism of others • Social withdrawal • Rage • Binge eating • Binge drinking • Impulsivity • Using drugs • Harming oneself or others	• Headaches • Crying • Fatigue • Weight loss/ gain • Insomnia • Teeth clenching • Increase in sweating • Exhaustion • Indigestion • Tremors

If you recognize any of these symptoms suddenly appearing in your life, it is probably the result of stress. However, chronic stress can cause these problems to become chronic as well and can cause damage that is not easily undone. If stress is constantly a problem in your life, we hope that you change the way you manage stress, thus changing the energy you put out to the universe so that you may get relief from stress.

Earlier in the book we talked about how important it is to reduce stress from a health standpoint. Stress has a major impact on your daily health and also on your lifespan (Taylor et al., 2000), as you can see in the chart above. Doctors and researchers are not sure if stress is a risk factor in heart disease or if having a lot of stress in your life can worsen other risk factors, such as blood pressure and cholesterol. Whether stress can directly or indirectly cause heart disease remains debatable, but research shows that optimistic men are fifty percent less likely to die from heart disease than those less hopeful (*London Times,* 2006). Doctors agree that there is a link between stress and heart disease and that because of this relationship, you should do all that you can in order to manage stress in your life in a positive way (WebMD).

Stress is also the result of negative thoughts and emotions. When you feel stressed, it is often because something has happened that you did not want to happen, or conversely, that something did not happen that you wanted to happen. Unfortunately, you are not always in control of things that happen around you; the stress that results from external factors is situational stress. For example, if you are in a car accident, you may feel physical, mental, emotional, and financial stress. This car accident was out of your control, but you can learn to cope with the stresses associated with it. You know that with time, you will heal and calm yourself down, and you will have your car fixed. To cope with the stress of a car accident, or any other stress that results from external factors, it is most helpful to change your thoughts and emotions about the situation as quickly as possible and feel confident that the LOA will help everything work out for the best in any situation.

Oftentimes stress can also be the result of the build-up of a lot of things that may not have worked out the way you expected or wanted. For example, many people cite finances as a cause of stress in their lives. Perhaps you have $50 thousand in credit card debt. Each month you expect to spend less, earn more, and start to pay off the debt. Yet every month, you continue to be disappointed by your inability to do so. You keep thinking things will change, but they do not. This problem must be tackled from several different angles because, just as it took time to accumulate $50 thousand in debt, it is going to take time to diminish the debt and reduce the stress associated with the debt. The first step is to deal with the short-term stress: the sense of panic that creeps up every time you think about the debt. This can be accomplished by changing negative thoughts, feelings, and actions into positive ones. You must fully believe that you can reduce this debt and take actions that will help your financial situation. If you need to make more money, figure out a plan that will help you make more money and stick with it. If you need to cut your spending, sit down and find ways that you can realistically cut back.

Positive actions lead to positive results. You want to be free of financial stress, so you must take positive actions and believe you can do it. Remember, positive actions create vibrations that the universe will pay attention to. Doing nothing and continuing to spend more and save less will create more stress and the LOA will work against you, bringing you more debt.

Another form of stress that everyone has in their lives is the feeling of being overwhelmed by the many responsibilities we have on a daily, weekly, or monthly basis, which is often accompanied by the feeling that there are not enough hours in a day to accomplish everything that needs to be done. We refer to this as time stress. You'll never guess what causes it...you! You may not want to accept this, but if you find yourself constantly feeling that there is not enough time in your day to accomplish the things you need to, then you are not managing your time as best you can, and you may have to take a fresh look at your responsibilities. You may say, "But things come up and sometimes I am unable to get to what I really needed to do." Yes, this is true. However, instead of feeling stressed about what you did not do, using the LOA, your focus should be on all that you were able to accomplish during the day. This will reduce the negative effects of stress in your life.

For many people, work contributes a great deal of stress to their lives. Ask yourself what you can do to improve your work-related stress. A study found that reorganization at work is a major source of stress prevention (Karasek, 2004). You can look at ways to reorganize what you do with your job and thereby reduce the amount of stress that appears in your life by preventing it from occurring in the first place, if possible.

Time management is all about prioritizing, and this is also a key strategy in managing your time stress. We suggest you do a simple exercise every morning for one to two weeks. When you wake up in the morning, take out a sheet of paper and draw three columns. In the first column, make a list of things that are important for you to accomplish during that day. You should number the items in order of importance. In the second column, state the reason why this particular item is so important. In the third column, estimate how long it will take to complete. We suggest you keep your list rather short and each item rather general. The reason why is that by keeping your list short, you are more likely to accomplish everything on it. Also, keep in mind that this is an exercise intended to help you connect with the things in your life that are the most important and to help you realize that you are doing a great job of accomplishing the important things. Following is an example:

Now let's analyze this list. It is short. These are all relatively simple things to accomplish, but all are very important.

1. You go to work to provide for your family and your future. Yes, there are many things to accomplish at work, but in the grand scheme of things, the most important thing is that you go to work and spend that time earning money.

2. Getting a full night's sleep is not always going to happen, but if you make it a priority and you do get a full night of sleep, you will most likely function and feel better because of it. Sleeping is something you must do anyway, why not feel a sense of accomplishment about it?

1. Go to work	Working allows me to earn money and provide for my future.	9 hours
2. Get 8 hours of sleep	Getting a full night's sleep will greatly improve my mood and well-being.	8 hours
3. Tell my spouse and children that I love and appreciate them	They mean a lot to me and I want them to know that.	10 minutes
4. Go to the grocery store	We need food to eat.	1 hour
5. Clean out the refrigerator when loading in the new groceries	It needs cleaning out.	10 minutes

3. Telling the people around you how much you care about them can take just a few minutes, yet it can mean so much. Further, if you have told them how you feel, then you do not have to question whether you showed them how you feel that day.

4. A routine chore like picking up food at the grocery store is something that you have to do often, but it is very important because you have to eat.

5. Cleaning out your refrigerator is not really as important as the other items on your list, but it is something you know needs to be done. If it does not get done, so what? You will get to it eventually if it does not get done today, but if you do clean out the fridge, then you should feel good about it. You can make a goal of number five being something that really is not that important but that you have on your agenda and you want to get done. That way, if you do not get around to it you can easily brush it off, but if you do get it done, you can feel a sense of accomplishment.

Think about what other areas of your life may need stress relief. We have just given you two examples: finances and time management, two major sources of stress. The first step in relieving stress in your life is figuring out what aspects of your life contributing to your stress. Perhaps your stress is a result of relationships with others, your job, your health, someone else's health, or your need for organization. Figure out what stresses most need to be eliminated from your life and ask for resolutions to them every single day. Also keep in mind that you will begin to notice that once you really start changing your negative thoughts into positive thoughts, the stress that you have in your life will start to diminish. The stress you experience every day is in your control and you can turn stress into peace. Stress is turmoil. Your goal is relaxation and peace within yourself and your life.

15

Success

The successful always has a number of projects planned to which he looks forward. Anyone of them could change the course of his life overnight.

—Mark Caine

Success can either mean accomplishing a goal or reaching a level of social status. For every unique individual in existence, the specific definition of success is different. Remember, just because society deems financial success, fame, and status to be signs of success does not mean you have to as well. The LOA is all about getting what you want. Whatever makes you feel like a success is what you should expect to achieve. It is important to ask the universe for the specific things you need in order to make your idea of success a reality, as well as asking for success itself. Changing your thoughts and feelings to positive ones will also help you achieve success while also improving your approach to achieving it on a daily basis. It has been shown that happiness is associated with and precedes numerous successful outcomes as well as behaviors paralleling success (Lyubomirsky et al., 2005). It has also been shown that taking a strategic approach in improving yourself can have dramatic effects on your long-term success (Robson & Hansson, 2007).

Many people seek fortune to become a success. Money can buy you many things and can make certain aspects of life easier. It is helpful to remember that fortune is a subjective amount. If success is constituted by a quantifiable amount of money in your mind, you must ask yourself how much exactly it will take for you to be satisfied. Set an amount in your head and use the LOA, as described in previous chapters, to reach that amount.

Fame is another form of success. Perhaps you want to be known in a positive light by the entire world, and further, respected for what you do. Do you have a particular talent that will get you there? Maybe acting, singing, journalism, or radio hosting is your passion. Imagine yourself doing these things and getting positive attention from hundreds, thousands, or even millions of people, if this is what you want! Picture yourself climbing the ladder of success, gaining more and more fame as you move up the ladder. You can do whatever it is that you want. You can be whatever you want to be. The LOA will help you get there. If fame is what you seek, then visualize yourself becoming famous!

Perhaps you do not want to be famous, but you do want respect. For example, an artist might want to become well known among a small group of people or a researcher might want accolades from colleagues and peers that he respects. You want to be seen as a success, both in your eyes and the eyes of those around you who you admire and respect. Everyone wants to be appreciated and do good work. You can accomplish this form of success by allowing the LOA to work for you.

Many parents see their success through their children. Although it is a wonderful goal to try and be the best parent you can be for your child, it is also important to remember that you are only in control of your own feelings and behavior. You can aim to be successful in your role of being a parent—making good decisions and being supportive of your children—but you cannot take credit for the successes or the failures your children experience. Many parents say that they want to raise successful children, but realize that your definition of success may be different from their definitions, when they one day have their own definitions. You must have confidence in their abilities and not in their success itself.

Fear of success is very common in many of you who are reading this book right now. Fear of success often translates into fear of the unknown. You know that you want to be successful, but you do not know what comes with that success. We fear that which we do not know. You may want to feel the positive aspects of your future success, but you may also be scared or fearful of what negative changes might occur along with it. This can be overcome. The good news is that the entire process we have outlined in this book will help you overcome your fear of success. The act of figuring out what you do and do not want from the universe serves to concurrently help you identify in which areas of your life you most wish for success.

Also, be aware that the act of asking and allowing the universe to grant these successes to you only creates vibrations when you truly want them to happen. Changing your thought processes, your feelings and behavior to focus on the positive will help you overcome your fear of success so that you can allow success to enter your life. Only when you truly allow and desire success in your life, free of any and all fears, will the successes be granted to you by the universe. Below is a sample script that Steve uses with his clients who fear success. You can use this script as a daily affirmation to help get over your fear of success.

> I realize that I am worthy of success. I deserve to be successful. I see it. I feel it. I see and feel success. I imagine myself successful. I notice what is surrounding me. I notice my environment. I see where I live and I am successful. I see how I live a successful life. I see how others treat me and how I am respectful to others. I am a wonderful person and I deserve this success. It feels so good to be successful in all areas of my life, mentally, physically, spiritually, financially, emotionally, in all of the areas in my life…successful. I see and feel myself as being successful. And I realize that I will maintain my success. I will continue to be a successful person because my success is a positive event for all of the people in my life. I set an example of how people should and can live, how they can reach their full potential. My success benefits everyone in my life, because by seeing myself as a successful person, it helps others realize their own potential. So by being successful, I benefit everyone in my life. I realize how much I deserve to be successful. I deserve it 100 percent. I deserve to be successful and as I breathe in deeply now, I breathe in strength and courage, and as I exhale, I let go of fear. And as I breathe in, I breathe in worthiness. I am worthy of all the good things life has to offer. And as I exhale, I let go of all the rest of my fear, I let it go. I am a successful person, I feel it. I feel it deep down inside. I have always understood deep down inside that I deserve to be successful, and now I realize that it is absolutely true. It is my destiny to be successful and to maintain and increase that success. So now I relax and I realize that I am successful and I will continue to increase my success day by day by, taking those steps necessary to increase my success. And I take those steps in a very powerful way because I deserve to be successful. I relax and realize just how successful I am and how much more successful I will become because I deserve to be successful.

Another aspect of success that often pushes people away from reaching their goal is the fear of failure. Fear of failure can be incapacitating and can prevent success from being achieved. It prevents people from going after their goals and dreams. It can be completely immobilizing for some. Some people are so scared to go after what they want simply because they are scared they may fail at it. Caraway, Ticker, Reinke, & Hall (2003) found through their research that the fear of failure is often instilled at a young age, has a negative impact on the ability to succeed, and can have long-term negative effects unless you realize it is an issue in your life. Fear of failure is common, but we are going to help you by giving you the tools to help you to overcome it.

First, it may be helpful to realize that simply following the LOA will help you overcome your fear of failure. When you recognize what it is you truly want from the universe, you will likely take steps to make it happen. The first step in overcoming the fear of failure is to take action. Find out what it is that you want in life. You are in the middle of this process right now. Figuring out what you want and what will help you become successful in your life is the first step in overcoming your fear of failure.

Second, do not give up! Keep asking for what you want from the universe. You know what you want, so ask for it and expect to receive it from the universe. You deserve to lead a life free of the fear of failure. Being persistent in your quest will help you immensely. It is important to keep an open mind as well as have patience with the LOA. You must take action and risk failure in order to achieve success.

Another aspect that will help you overcome fear of failure is changing your mindset. Above all, you should try to not focus on past mistakes and negative events as failures. Certainly you have learned something from past mistakes, so you cannot view them as complete failures. Now is the time to eradicate negative events from your mind. For a few minutes, think of the ways in which you benefited in some way from a negative event. Then, erase all other aspects about the negative event from your mind without giving it a second thought.

Below is another script that Steve uses with his patients to help them overcome their fear of failure. Use this script as a daytime affirmation to help overcome fear of failure. We believe this will help you on your way to being a success!

I realize just how powerful I am. I am an amazing person. I am now going to take a moment and just reflect on all the wonderful, amazing things about myself. My creativity, my intelligence, my sense of adventure, my desire to succeed, my acceptance of myself. All of these things make me such a wonderful, beautiful person. I realize now just how wonderful and powerful I am, and as I breathe in deeply now, I breathe in confidence. And as I exhale, I let go of any uncertainty, let it go. And breathing in again, I breathe in motivation and power. And as I exhale, I let go of doubt, let it go, and I let go of fear, let it go. I am so relaxed and at ease and confident. Now I imagine a goal or project, something I would like to accomplish. And I imagine already having accomplished it. I see myself there, accomplishing my goal. I feel powerful. I am relaxed. It seems so easy to have accomplished it. I now remember all the steps that went toward accomplishing my goal or project, and I notice that along the way, there were some situations that were challenging. And I notice how I dealt with those situations, easily and effortlessly, in a very relaxed way. I realize that with any goal, there are challenges, and I am always up to the challenge. I am relaxed and confident, relaxed and confident. And I see those challenges as necessary steps, and I deal with those challenges very quickly and efficiently, very quickly and efficiently, as if I were a gladiator. And those challenges are very easy to defeat, very easy to defeat because I am a mighty gladiator and I am able to defeat any challenge that may arise easily and effortlessly. And as I breathe in deeply now, I breathe in strength and courage. And as I exhale slowly, I let go of fear, I let it go, let it go, let it go. I am able to accomplish anything I choose to accomplish. Any goal or project I wish to accomplish, I will accomplish easily, meeting all the challenges along the way. And now I look to the future. I look to that time when I have finished that goal. And I see a clear path now, I see the challenges, but I remember how I overcame them easily and efficiently. And I realize now that there is a clear path to my goal. And I will now walk that path easily, letting go of fear, breathing in strength, breathing in that strength and courage. And as I exhale, I let go of fear, I let it go. I am a mighty warrior and I will reach my goal and I will reach my goal easily.

16

Career

*Climbing to the top demands strength, whether it is to the top
of Mount Everest or to the top of your career.*

—Abdul Kalam

You can attract great things to your job or your career. You can get
the job you have been dreaming of; you can be your own boss; you
can enjoy the people you work with. You can get satisfaction from the
work that you do, no matter what it is. You can make your financial
goals match your career goals.

The first question you should ask yourself is whether you are in the
right job or career for you. Then ask yourself which of these three
options most applies to you:

A. I am happy with my job and do not want to change.
B. I am not completely pleased with my job, but I want to be happy
   where I am.
C. I am not happy with my job and I want to do something else.

You may be thinking that your situation is more complicated than
this. Yes, life may seem complicated, but at times, it is only as complicated as you make it. Choose a different option that is tailored to your
own situation, but for the most part, you can probably summarize
your situation with your job or career into the above three options.

Remember, there are no excuses for why you have the job that you
have. Having the frame of mind that you are "stuck" in your job will
only leave you feeling worthless.

This next section will show you how you can change this with the Law of Attraction. We assume that you want to change your feelings, if they are in fact negative, about your job, since spending many hours in a position that you do not like can have a variety of negative effects on your well-being. For example, Paivandy, Bullock, Reardon, & Kelly (2008) found that negative thoughts about one's career have a negative impact on decision-making ability.

If you answered **A** to the above career statements, congratulations! Having a rewarding career that makes you happy is truly a wonderful feeling. You probably have a positive mindset when it comes to your job, and we encourage you to keep finding the positive in what you do. Even people who are unhappy with their careers make it a goal to attain enjoyment in their jobs, often taking a lot of time to do so. You can feel empowered by your enjoyment of your job but still use the LOA to enhance other aspects of your life.

Remember, since you are happy with you job or career, it is important that you be sincerely thankful for it and the happiness it brings you. In your career, the LOA is already working for you. Whatever you are doing in regard to your career and the LOA, it is aligning with the universe, and you are creating positive energy. Make sure that you continue to stay happy in your job because the universe will take notice, helping you achieve abundance in other areas of your life.

Perhaps you most identify with statement **B**, the most common choice. Perhaps there are aspects of your career that are not great, but given your current life circumstances, you feel the need to stay put and make the best of things. Situation B is a good thing! You do not need to change jobs; you simply need to change your focus and your mindset in order to get more pleasure out of your situation. Change your focus from the things you do not like about your job to those you do like, and turn your thoughts to the good things about it, rather than the negative. It is important to your career and yourself that you change dysfunctional career thoughts into positive ones (Van Ecke, 2007).

Perhaps you like certain tasks that you are responsible for. Maybe you enjoy the time you spend with co-workers. Maybe you like your pay and benefits. If you identify with statement B, then all you have to do is make a concerted effort to change how you think and feel about your job. Find and focus on the good and positive aspects of your job and soon you will start gaining more enjoyment from your job.

An exercise we suggest to help improve your outlook on your job is to incorporate visualization. Imagine getting enjoyment from tasks you used to find difficult, tedious, or unenjoyable. Remember to ask the universe for happiness in your career. You want to be happy with your current job, and you deserve to be happy with your current job. Allow that happiness to show itself to you. Throughout your work day, appreciate the things you do and tell yourself you are doing a great job. You should be your own biggest supporter.

It is also important to focus on future goals. Imagine getting great satisfaction from your job. Focusing on the future and positive results will make you more likely to feel enjoyment at work, which is your ultimate goal. You can choose to find your job or career rewarding. You can identify the positive aspects of your job and focus on those. If you want to stay in your job, then a positive outlook is what you should have.

On the other hand, if you want to make a career change, then there are many more areas to explore. For those of you who categorize your job situation as statement **C**, you can immediately start using the LOA to attract your ideal job or career! Look at this time in your life as an exciting opportunity. Your ultimate goal in changing careers is to find enjoyment in what you do on a daily basis. Every day that you work at this is another day you become closer to accomplishing the goal of working in your ideal career.

If you need to change jobs or careers, it is important to keep a positive attitude. Changing jobs can be viewed as either stressful or exciting. You must choose to remain positive throughout the transition. The ultimate goal in this case is for you to be happy with your new career. When you think about it, your job and career take up a majority of your waking hours. Therefore, it is of the utmost importance that you enjoy what you do. An important question to ask yourself is, "What is my ideal career?" Perhaps you already know in the back of your mind what you would really like to do. If you already know what you want to do, ask yourself what steps you need to take in order to make it happen. Formulate a plan. Think about what you need to do and write it all down. Whether you need to find an open position through networking or start building a business from scratch, think about what you need to do to get that position or career.

Perhaps you are not quite sure what you want to do. If so, then we encourage you to explore and research different jobs and careers to find out what will work for you. We also suggest that you interview for different jobs and ask a lot of questions to make sure that you are doing all that you can to find the right fit. Finding the right job for you is something only you can do. In order to attract your ideal career, you have to be happy with your choice in order to create positive vibrations for the universe. You must, for the most part, ignore other people's opinions on what you should do for a career. Only you know what will truly make you happy.

Perhaps your ideal career is to start your own business, where you are the boss and you have complete control. Obviously, we the authors are both familiar with starting our own businesses, but we did not know much at all when we first started. We have learned along the way. We both have experienced failure, but we learned from it and have turned them into success. We do not see it as failure because we were able to overcome it and learn from our mistakes.

The key to running your own business is having drive and motivation. If owning your own company is your goal, then we suggest you ask the universe for motivation. When you find your true calling, the motivation is going to come along with it, as a result of you desiring it, having asked for it and allowed it in.

In order to make the LOA really work for you insofar as career is concerned, you should be able to answer the following questions: What do you want to do? How many hours do you want to work a week? How many employees do you want to have? Imagine yourself performing a job and enjoying it and being good at it! Picture yourself running a business. See yourself with customers or clients. See yourself allocating tasks and having people work for you. Realize the enjoyment and satisfaction you have by being your own boss. You can take off when you want to. You make all the rules. Imagine all the details. Come up with new details of your own. Picture it every day.

We found that this was an extremely important step in our own processes. We envisioned exactly what we wanted. One of the things that we both wanted was to be our own bosses. We wanted to call the shots for our own companies. We envisioned having this a long time before either one of us was actually able to begin our own company. We felt the desire to make this a reality. Every day we would envision it in our minds. We knew what it felt like, the joy and the freedom that it brought to us. This is different for everyone because everyone wants something different. One person may want a brand new car whereas someone else may want a better career for himself or herself. Everyone's desires are going to be different in this process.

Following is a script Steve uses with clients who are trying to find their ideal jobs. This is meant as an exercise to help you find out what your true calling is. Take your time reading the excerpt below and imagine different careers as you read. You may want to read the script several times.

I imagine myself sitting in front of several television sets. There may be five, ten, or twenty, or a hundred, however many as I choose to see. On each of these television sets I see myself performing a different job. There are many things that I am capable of doing. Yet, there are only a few that will lead to my ultimate satisfaction and allow me to achieve the goals I have in life and allow me to fulfill my destiny and do what I am meant to do. As I watch myself perform these various jobs on these television sets, if I see myself performing a job which does not measure up to my criteria, my own criteria of what is good for me, of what makes me feel good about myself, I turn that television off. As I go through this exercise I notice television sets being turned off every now and then because as I zero in and focus on my perfect job, I find that the other jobs just do not measure up. Certainly I can perform them, but for whatever reason they are not what I am meant to do. I now turn off all the television sets which show me doing something that I really do not like doing. Any of the television sets displaying me performing a job that I really do not like doing; I am turning them off right now. Now I am turning off any television sets that show me doing something that someone else wants me to do, which I only partially want to do—turning them off. Occasionally certain television sets will come back on, showing me doing something different. So now I turn on certain television sets that show me doing a job that I would love to do but that I used to think I couldn't do. I see those television sets coming on now. It can be any job at all. The possibilities are endless, any job. I imagine myself doing any job at all; any job that I want to do even if I previously thought that I could not. I now turn off any television sets that show myself doing a job that I do not think will lead me to the level of financial satisfaction that I desire. I turn those television sets off now. I also turn off any television sets that show myself doing a job that I really know that I should not be doing; any job that my conscience tells me not to do. I tune in now to my conscience. My conscience is what tells me right from wrong. We all have one. Certainly, there is no such thing as an absolute right and wrong, but I have an internal compass that tells me my truth, what is right and what is wrong for me. So now I turn off any television sets that show me doing a job that is wrong for me. I am now thinking of other jobs I can do. As these ideas come to me, I allow those television sets to turn back on, showing me performing that new job that I just thought of. I am now freezing the remaining television sets that are on. No matter how many or how few television sets are on, I just freeze them with the current picture they show. I give them all labels. I take my time, labeling each one, simple labels, big labels that I can read easily; or perhaps I can hear those labels if I am more of an auditory person. So now I can either see the labels on those various jobs or hear the labels. Either way, I finish up now and label the rest of the jobs. Now, no matter how many jobs are in front of me, I narrow them down to no more than ten. I tap into my gut reaction and get rid of all of them except ten. Whichever ones I want to eliminate first, I eliminate, so that I am left with only ten jobs. Now, I narrow it down to no more than five jobs, five jobs maximum. If the number is not already five or fewer, I eliminate any that are beyond five. Just the ones that I feel I should eliminate. And now I have a maximum of five jobs in front of me. The goal of this exercise is to find my perfect job. One job that is perfect for me, one of the remaining jobs. Now I eliminate all but two of the jobs in front of me. One of them appeals to me more than the other. I choose that one now, the one that appeals to me more, I just do it, I do not think, I just go with my instinct. And as I do so, the other one disappears and all the other television sets go away so that I just see myself doing that one job. That television set becomes louder and brighter, and it begins to show me in various scenes doing that job. I embrace this job now and realize that I am going to move toward getting this job in my life. This is the perfect job for me, and I will do everything I can to make this job happen.

Now, I see myself in the future, at the time when I have this job. Certainly, it could be a professional job that could take me a while to obtain, and that's fine. I see myself in the future doing that job, and as I look back now at the present, I see all the simple, easy, logical steps that had to happen for me to get that job. I see how easy they are as I look at them from the future. I see myself in that job, perhaps wearing that uniform, wearing whatever clothes I wear for that job. My perfect job feels wonderful. I am a part of it now. This is my future. And as I move back now to the present, I realize that I will get this perfect job if I do not already have it. I will take the steps necessary to get this perfect job and fulfill my destiny. I am very happy with myself because I have done what so few people do. I have made a powerful decision for my future. So now I will go get that job. I go and take the steps necessary to get that job. I make it fun and exciting and multi-dimensional. I think of new skills I can learn in this job. I congratulate myself and relax because everything is going to be just fine.

We hope that this exercise helps you in your quest to find your perfect career!

The key to changing careers or starting your own business is the LOA and using everything we already have and will continue to outline in this book. Knowing what you want and going after it is of utmost important in this process. Find a career that is right for you. Ask for a position to open up or ask that you be fruitful in entrepreneurial endeavours. Allow yourself to find your career and become successful. When the LOA works for you and you receive what you have been asking for, then enjoy it, cherish it and be grateful for it! You deserve to be happy in your work.

17

Things

We all want *things*. You may have been first introduced to the concept of the LOA on the basis of attracting things. There are so many different items that people want—obviously we cannot list them all here—but there are some bigger items that almost everyone wants to attract in a general sense and we will be using some of those as examples.

You can attract things using the same method you are using to attract everything else that you want. You must visualize the items, ask for them, allow them to enter your life, receive them, and then be thankful for them. You'll want to pretend as if you already have the items, and imagine what it is like. The key here is to immerse your life with the items that you want. You want to eat, sleep, think, feel, and behave with these items on your brain.

What is it that you want? If you could have anything in the world, what would be on your list? Start by writing down those things that you desire. Writing down exactly what you want puts you one step closer to attracting it. We suggest that you start by listing about five items that you want, and as you receive them, add another item onto your list. By doing this, in effect you will be constantly accumulating more things that you want. We also suggest that you carry this list around on a small piece of paper at all times throughout the day you can be constantly reminded of these items. You can also make this list and store it in random places such as a document on your computer, perhaps even both your personal and work computers. You can write the list and leave the piece of paper on your refrigerator. You can keep a list next to your bed or use it as a bookmark. Make several of these lists so that you can constantly be reminded of what you will one day attract.

It is important that while using this process you do not view this list of items as things you have not yet received but rather as things you will have soon. It is also important to remain positive, to know that these items will come into your life, and to allow these things into your life. When you look at your list or think of your list in your head, you should smile and imagine your life with those items. Your focus should be on what it would be like to have them and how they would contribute to your overall happiness.

Sometimes people have trouble connecting the universe with things in this step. People tend to understand how the LOA can deliver feelings and concepts such as happiness and wealth into their lives but are unsure of how the universe will deliver a car. Remember, anything and everything is possible with the LOA. If you want a house and you are completely aligned with receiving a house in your life, the universe will make it happen for you. The same goes for all other things you could possibly want from the universe.

HOUSE

Most people want to own a house or condominium because it is something to call their own and because it is an investment or an achievement. Owning a house is a great accomplishment. The mortgage payment becomes a monthly investment, unlike renting. If you rent, we encourage you to aim for owning a house if you plan on staying in one place for the long term. If you already own a house, you may want a bigger and better house or possibly a second home. Your house is a symbol of your success and it is the one place in the world you can call your own.

Do you want a better home for yourself? If so, how many rooms do you want? What is the exact location of the home? What do the rooms look like? What are the colors of the walls? How many windows are there? Does the home have a swimming pool? Does it have a driveway? These are examples of the specific types of questions you must ask yourself when deciding on what you want.

Let us look at an example of how you can use the LOA to attract your ideal home. If you want a nicer home, find a picture of that home and carry it with you or post it in a place where you will see it every day to surround yourself with this intention as a reality. Take time out of your day to look at it as often as you can. Surrounding yourself with your dreams and intentions is the most powerful step in using the LOA to its fullest potential.

Imagine what your dream house would be like. It can be your first home, a second home, or your next home. Below is a list of characteristics to consider when imagining your dream home. Take time to consider each item and imagine specific features of your house:

- Location: In what area of the world? In what town or city? In a residential neighborhood? In a high-rise building?
- Size of property: Is your home on a small or large piece of land?
- Size of house: How many square feet? How many stories?
- Yard: What does the yard look like? Is there a lot of grass or wooded area? Is there no yard? Is there a swing set? A dock? Outdoor area for entertaining?
- View: Does your house have a view of a mountain, prairie, beach, river, marsh, or city skyline?
- Exterior: What does your house look like on the outside? What color is it? What do the windows and the roof look like? Imagine circling around the house. What do you see?
- Number of bedrooms: How many bedrooms do you want your home to have?
- Rooms: What does the kitchen look like? What does the family room look like? Does your house also have a dining room, office, playroom, exercise room, porch, garage, tool shed, and basement? Imagine the different rooms, the colors of the walls, the nice fixtures and flooring, and any items inside the house.
- Bathrooms: How many bathrooms? What do they look like?
- What does it feel like to be in your house? How does it make you feel?
- What does it smell like inside your home?
- What do you want to occur in your house? Do you want to raise a family? Entertain? Showcase a talent?

Imagine any and all details that you can. Add any more details you want to this list in order to make your dream house a reality. Remember, anything is possible. If it helps you to imagine your perfect house, write down all the details. Many visual people find it helpful to make a list of all the details of their house or even draw a picture of what they are imagining. Whether you are visual or not, we suggest you create or find a picture of your dream house and put it in a box, on your refrigerator, or any place you want that will keep it in the forefront of your mind. Having a visual reminder of your dream house is a powerful signal to the universe.

Once you have created in your mind or found a picture of your ideal house, imagine that it is your own. For a few minutes every day, close your eyes and imagine living your life inside that house. Imagine waking up in the morning in your bedroom. Imagine cooking in the kitchen or watching TV in the family room or playing with your kids in the backyard. Imagine it being yours for at least two minutes every day. Picture yourself in your house, enjoying yourself and really getting a sense of what it would be like to live there. Immerse yourself in this visualization. Imagine what it looks like, feels like, smells like, and how it sounds. Try to involve your senses whenever possible every time you create the visualization of your dream house.

Car

Most of you would probably like to drive a different car. What is one of the best ways to find out what car you want? Go for a test drive! You can go to different car dealerships and look at, touch, and drive the different cars available. Perhaps you want a small car that drives fast and fits in any parking spot. Maybe you want a large sport-utility vehicle to hold a lot of things or carry a lot of people. Maybe you want a truck to haul things. Maybe you want an energy-efficient vehicle that will be better for the environment or cheaper on gas. The important thing to figure out first is the kind of car you want.

After you have figured out the make and model of your future car, the next thing to do is to figure out which of the many features available you want your car to possess. What is important to you? Seat warmers? Swanky rims? Safety features? There are even cars now that can parallel park themselves—maybe you want that as well. Imagine any and all details that you can picture. Leather or cloth seats? What color is the interior? What color is the outside? How spacious is the trunk area? Is there a sunroof? How many cylinders and horsepower? What kind of gas mileage does it get? How does it feel to sit in the car and drive it? Once you identify your ideal car, we suggest you either take a picture of one that you see out on the road or cut a picture out of a magazine. It is important to have a specific car in mind when using the LOA. This way you know exactly what you want, the universe knows exactly what you want, and in a matter of time you will attract your ideal car.

An exercise you can do to help attract your perfect car is to imagine that your current car is your ideal car. Whenever you are driving, imagine that you are already driving your dream car. Picture all the details, such as the color of the car on both the inside and outside while you are driving. Imagine people looking at you in your fancy car (if that is what you want). Imagine your kids entertaining themselves with the TV in the back of your SUV. Imagine a quiet ride and low emissions in a hybrid vehicle. The possibilities are endless. This visualization technique will help you create vibrations in line with the universe!

NICE THINGS

We are grouping everything else into one category because everyone has unique wants and different tastes. Some people want to live a life of luxury and surround themselves with fancy and expensive things. Some people wish to keep their life simple and may only want to attract a few things into their lives. Most of you will be somewhere in between. Below is a list of things to consider asking the universe for. Remember, your options are truly limitless!

- Clothes
- Jewelry
- Watches
- TVs, computers, electronics
- Appliances
- Furniture
- Motorcycles
- Boats
- Country club membership
- Art
- Hobbies

18

Lifestyle

Lifestyle intervention requires discipline with a tangible end result that is within reach. It requires personal resolve, a lifelong commitment.

—Tim Holden

We have now come to the final topic of attraction, and that is lifestyle. Often you will find that the other topics we have focused on in this book, such as happiness, wealth, and physical things, contribute to or are important to a certain lifestyle. The way we live our lives has a major impact on the other aspects, such as happiness and success. **They are interchangeable.** Your lifestyle choices have a direct impact on everything else that occurs in your life. You can use the LOA to attract a healthier lifestyle, a more leisurely lifestyle, or a more organized lifestyle.

The first topic in relation to lifestyle that we will talk about is a healthy lifestyle. We are not talking about your health, but rather the habits that affect your health. There are many aspects to a healthy lifestyle, and you should strive to allow the LOA help you in leading one.

EATING RIGHT

A healthy lifestyle includes eating right. We all know what we *should* be eating, but often we do not engage in healthy eating habits. Eating foods that are unhealthy sends out negative messages to the universe, such as, "I do not care enough for my health to put nutritious food in my body" and "I would rather receive the short-term benefits of tasting this food than receive the long-term benefits of nutritious food." These are negative things that you indirectly communicate to the universe when you eat and/or drink unhealthy things. This does not mean that you have to completely expel unhealthy foods from your diet. However, only eating unhealthy foods once in a while and in moderation will tell the universe that you respect your body and your health.

Weight is a major issue for many people these days. Doctors and the news continually makes us aware of what carrying extra weight on our bodies can and will do to us down the road. We hear statistics all the time from new studies. The issue of weight constantly bombards us, so it makes sense that we would want to attract a healthy lifestyle and healthy eating habits into our lives. We the authors both believe in the power of eating right and we have both made changes in our diets during our adult lives that have had profound effects on our overall lifestyle. The fact of the matter is that most people want to be at a healthy weight, and the only way to do that is by living a healthy lifestyle.

One way to attract healthy eating habits is by changing the way you eat and view food. You'll want to change your mindset and see healthy foods as appetizing instead of junk foods. We suggest this technique: Imagine your refrigerator filled with healthy and delicious foods that you enjoy. In your mind, put good, quality, healthy foods into your "mental refrigerator." See your refrigerator filled with fruits, vegetables, lean meats, and natural foods. When you think about the next meal you are going to eat, think about how much pleasure you are going to get from the healthy food on your plate. You can change your eating habits. The LOA will help you with the process.

To help you see food as a friend and not as the enemy, we have provided affirmations to help you see food as fuel. Food is meant to fuel your system so that you feel your best all the time and your body and mind run at optimal performance. What you put into your body has a major impact on how you feel. Use the script below to help you change your eating habits by only eating food that fuels your body.

I picture my body as an engine. I know that the more I drive, the more gasoline I need. Our bodies are similar to an engine—the more I use my body, the more food it needs. If I am always on the go, moving around, exercising, and very active, I am going to need more food than someone who sits at a desk most of the day and does not move a lot. Just like an engine needs gasoline, I need the proper sources of food to keep me going. I would not put water, juice, or coffee in my car, as my car would not run properly or at all. I must eat healthy foods in order to be healthy, mentally sharp, and have enough energy to get me through the day. In order to use food as fuel, I must eat lean protein, whole grains, vegetables, and fruits. These are the best foods to get all the nutrients and minerals my body needs for optimal health and performance. Lean proteins consist of fish, poultry, beans, nuts, and soy. These are all high in protein, and protein will keep me satisfied for a long period of time. Protein stays in my body and gives me the energy I need so that I feel good throughout the day. Whole grains are important because they are an excellent source of carbohydrates. Carbohydrates also give me energy, but this energy is short term energy. It won't stay with me for a long period of time, but it will give me more of an instant boost. It is very important to balance protein and carbohydrates; both are very important. I want to eat whole grains because they have fiber, the part of carbohydrates that keeps me satisfied longer. Fiber is a very important part of my diet and keeps me healthy. Vegetables and fruits are important because they contain so many valuable nutrients. Protein and carbohydrates will get me through my day, but vegetables and fruits will give me the vitamins and nutrients to sustain a long and healthy life. The more brightly colored the fruits and vegetables, the better. The bright colors mean that they are rich in antioxidants and vitamins. I should also strive to eat dark leafy greens. They also provide many nutrients that I cannot get anywhere else. I picture myself eating these foods. I eat lean protein, whole grains, vegetables, and fruits. I am able to have the energy I need throughout the day. Whether I am training for a marathon, chasing my children around the house, or spending nine hours at work, I need proper nutrition. What I put into my body has a direct effect on how my body feels, thinks, and performs. I will feel satisfied and energetic with the right foods. By getting rid of fried foods and saturated fats I will feel better throughout my day and I will notice long-term changes. I may not notice a change right away in my mental capabilities, but using good foods to nourish my body will have a drastic effect on my mental health in the long run. Perhaps a lifetime of eating right can help fight against Alzheimer's disease and cancer. The right nutrition will also affect how my body performs in the short-term and long-term. I will feel like I am in better shape if I am consuming the right foods in the short term. In the long term, the correct foods will help me keep my bones, joints, and muscles in good working order so that I can remain mobile and feel good as I age. I have complete control over what foods I consume, which means I have a lot of control over how my body feels and my mind performs.

EXERCISE

Another aspect of living a healthy lifestyle is exercise. You may have heard it all before, but exercise has amazing benefits to your overall well being. Mentally, physically, and emotionally, exercise can help you lead an active and healthy lifestyle (Kruger, Kohl & Miles, 2008). The more frequently you exercise, the easier it becomes. When you exercise, your body releases endorphins that make you feel better—mentally, physically and emotionally. Exercise also allows you to give off positive energy. The universe rewards this positive energy in many ways, including giving back more energy to you. Exercise is a necessity in life, but it can sometimes be difficult to motivate yourself. Often it is not the exercise that is so difficult but rather building up the motivation to do something that that you may view as difficult. Exercise has such an enormous positive effect that we suggest you use the LOA to help incorporate it into your life in every way that you can.

Below we have included a script that Steve uses with his clients to help them enjoy exercise. Exercising is a mandatory part of life if you want to stay even moderately healthy. The hardest part for most people is building up the motivation and establishing a work out routine. By reading the below as a daytime affirmation, you will be helping yourself attract the love of exercise into your life.

> I realize that I love to exercise. I love to exercise. I love the results my body shows after I exercise. I love the act of exercising. I love learning how to exercise more efficiently. I love everything about exercise. I am so very relaxed when I think about exercising. I imagine myself right now exercising…and I see a smile on my face. I am really enjoying exercising. There are so many exercises I like to do. Choose one now and just focus on that one. I now imagine my body one year from now. And as I do that one exercise, I am very focused on how amazing and wonderful my body will look one year from now. My body is becoming more and more beautiful. My body is becoming more and more healthy and fit, more and more like what I want it to be day by day. I allow this to happen easily. As I see myself exercising I also see myself very focused on the beautiful body I am creating. I now imagine myself doing another exercise, so very focused, focused on creating a very healthy, very powerful, very fit body. And I realize that I am the sculptor of my own body. And I will sculpt it in any way I choose. By exercising, I sculpt my body. I create muscles the size that I want them to be and the proportion that I want them to be. I allow this to happen as I now imagine my ideal body. I

realize that I am working toward creating my ideal body and I allow it to happen. I realize that I love to exercise. I also love to relax and let my body rebuild itself. I also love proper nutrition. I love keeping my total body, mind, and spirit in perfect shape and day by day my love of exercise and my love of learning more about exercise grows.

You can repeat these affirmations to yourself once a day, a few times a day, or even while you are working out. Creating a positive outlook on exercise will help you attract the love of exercise into your life. Enjoying exercise may take time and will be made much easier by asking for help from the universe. As long as you stick to a regular exercise routine, the universe will take notice and exercise will get easier for you.

It is suggested by medical science that you get thirty minutes of exercise most days of the week (four or more days). Exercise is considered anything that continuously keeps your heart rate up for an extended amount of time. It is also good to generally be active for most of the day. It is suggested by doctors and researchers that you should take ten thousand steps every day. Leading an active lifestyle will give you more energy. The more energy you give out to the universe, the more you will get back. Being active and exercising gives out good and positive energy, telling the universe that you want more of it!

STOP SMOKING

If you are a smoker, you have heard how bad it is for you, thousands of times at the very least, and you have probably tried to quit on several occasions. Smoking is one of the worst things you can do to your body, and takes years off of your life. Every time you light up a cigarette and every time you take a puff, you are telling the universe you do not care about your body. We know you do not want to hear it, but if you smoke, you are using the LOA in a very negative way.

Quitting smoking is not going to be easy, but it is important to realize that you *can* quit. Steve has personally witnessed thousands of people successfully quit smoking with help from hypnosis. Whether you choose hypnotherapy or a different method, we want to encourage you to stop smoking. The U.S. Surgeon General said the following about stopping smoking: "Smoking cessation represents the single most important step that smokers can take to enhance the length and quality of their lives."

If you want to quit smoking, the LOA can help you get there. Use the tools we have outlined in this book. Choose a quit date. Steve usually asks clients to commit to a specific date three weeks in the future. Use the LOA to your benefit and ask the universe to help you quit once and for all. Every day, imagine your life without cigarettes. Imagine never wanting to smoke a cigarette again. Visualize a smoke-free environment. Create a new life in your mind that does not include cigarettes. Feel good about your decision. See the process of quitting as being easy and effortless. You have an amazing amount of will power. You are strong. You are vivacious. You owe it to yourself to stop smoking! Visualize your future as a non-smoker. Every day, imagine how good it feels to get rid of cigarettes from your life. You can do this!

If you smoke, the following affirmation will help you achieve your goal of becoming a non-smoker. Have faith in yourself, and remember—you are strong and you *can* quit smoking.

> Willingness is a state of mind, and I am willing to be a non-smoker because that is what I want. I will succeed. I am willing to do whatever it takes to produce the results I want. I choose to be a non-smoker. I am willing, willing to do whatever it takes to be a non-smoker. My thoughts create my behavior. When I have a behavior I want to change, I must change the thought pattern, and the behavior will change automatically. All of my behavior results directly from my thoughts. Therefore, I will think of myself as a non-smoker. I hear myself saying, "I am a non-smoker." When someone offers me a cigarette, I hear myself saying, "No thanks, I don't smoke." For my body, smoking is poison. I want to live a long and healthy life. I owe my body respect and protection. I have made a commitment to protect and respect my body, and when I do that, I then have the power within me to smoke my last cigarette. I will maintain my non-smoking easily and effortlessly. I hear myself repeating slowly in my mind, "I am a non-smoker now and forevermore. I am going to make this work. I expect this to work. I now allow myself to be a non-smoker. I deserve to be a non-smoker." I will maintain my non-smoking permanently. I will be relaxed when others are smoking around me. Cigarettes are poison. Cigarettes are filled with over four thousand substances that are harmful to my health. Now, when someone offers me a cigarette, I hear myself say, "No thank you, I quit." I am now and forever more a non-smoker. In the morning, before I can even open my eyes, I will tell myself, "I am strongly motivated to be a non-smoker, one day at a time, easily and effortlessly." I see myself going through my day and night without a cigarette. I see myself getting up in the morning with-

out a cigarette. I see myself having coffee or reading the paper, going through my morning without a cigarette. I see myself on the phone, without a cigarette. I see myself driving, playing my favorite music, relaxed and comfortable, without a cigarette. I see myself after a meal, without a cigarette. I am relaxed and comfortable, no interest, no desire for smoking. I see myself doing the things that I do throughout the day, whatever they may be, without a cigarette, uninterested, no desire. I see myself out with others, and someone lights up. I tell myself, cigarettes are not a sign of friendship. Cigarettes are poison. I am now and forevermore a non-smoker. Long ago there was a food that I decided not to eat. I imagine that food now. I made a decision that I would not eat that food and nothing and no one could make me pick up a fork and eat that disgusting and nauseating food. Just as now I have made my choice to be a non-smoker, and nothing and no one can make me take that first puff. Every time I look at a pack of cigarettes, I will think of that food and feel disgust, and nothing and no one can make me take the first puff. I am now and forever more a non-smoker. Now I recall a time in my life when I felt completely confident and proud of myself. I see that moment clearly. I notice the colors in the room. I hear the sounds associated with that event. I notice any odors associated with that event. I feel the atmosphere, my clothes, and the temperature. I now make all of those sounds, sights, and smells even more vivid and allow the feeling of pride associated with this event to build in intensity. And when I feel the pride associated with this event at the maximum level of intensity, I make a fist with my former smoking hand and as I hold the fist tightly, I take three slow deep breaths, in and out. I feel even more intensely the pride that I felt during the event. I am there now at that event. I feel that adrenaline rush as I breathe in and out now. I feel the sense of pride begin to get stronger. I now unclench my fist and relax even more deeply. I am now and forever more a non-smoker. If I ever feel an urge or a craving for a cigarette, I will make a fist with my former smoking hand. This is now my power hand. This is a signal to my subconscious mind that says I am powerful. I am a non-smoker. Now I take three deep breaths in and out. And as I exhale each time, I exhale my craving out into the atmosphere where it just dissipates and fades away. I will remember that if I feel a craving, I will make a fist and take three deep breaths. I will tell myself that a craving for a cigarette lasts for just a few seconds, and after I have done this, I can relax my hand. All I need to cope with is a few seconds, so I will distract myself. I think of the food I do not want to eat, and remember, this is not deprivation, this is reward. I will tell myself that I am not giving up pleasure, I am giving up poison. I tell myself the first puff is the problem. If I never take the first puff, I have no problem. I am now and forever more a non-smoker. I imagine myself one year from now. I am out with friends. I feel great. I look great. It has been a wonderful year. People around me are smoking. As I watch them puff away, I think about how lucky I am to be rid of that dirty, deadly habit. I hear someone offer me a cigarette. I hear myself say, "No thank you, I stopped smoking." I am now and forever more a non-smoker and every night before going to sleep, I tell myself, "I am a permanent non-smoker. I expect to be a non-smoker. I will allow myself to be a non-smoker. I deserve to be a non-smoker." I will relax, and let the results take care of themselves. I am a non-smoker. I have given up smoking for many reasons. I think of those reasons now. Clean, clear, healthy, pink lungs. More energy, more stamina. Clean smelling mouth. Clean smelling breath. To reinforce my confidence, to live a longer and healthy life and all the other good, positive, powerful reasons I have. I am now and forever more a non-smoker. No matter what is going on in my life, I am now and forever more a non-smoker. No matter how aggravated I may become, nothing and no one can make me take the first puff. No matter how upset and sad I can become at times, nothing and no one can make me take the first puff. No matter how heartbroken or aggravated I may be from time to time, nothing and no one can make me take the first puff. I believe it. I trust myself. A habit that is not fed is soon gone. I am now and forever more a non-smoker. Now all thoughts, all cravings, all urges connected to smoking are gone from my mind and my body. I will let it happen. I will let it happen easily and effortlessly. I have given up smoking for myself. I am now and forevermore a non-smoker.

This exercise will help you see yourself as a non-smoker. We suggest you repeat this every day, several times a day, before and after your quit date. Before you quit, repeating these affirmations will help you reinforce your reasons for quitting and help you see yourself in the future as a non-smoker. Repeating these affirmations after you quit will help you stay a non-smoker and will help you remain a non-smoker for the rest of your life.

OVERCOMING ADDICTIONS

Addictions can include a wide variety of things. Some of the most common addictions include alcohol, drugs, food, gambling, and sex. All of these addictions lead to negative lifestyles and can impact your life in a major way. An addiction includes excessive physical and/or psychological dependence on a substance. Addiction to alcohol and other drugs is the malignant disease of self. Addiction is a disease that is progressive and potentially fatal. It is not self curing (DuPont, 1997). Overcoming an addiction usually involves help from an outside source. It is fairly unlikely that you can do it on your own. If you suffer from an addiction, realize that you need help. Also, realize that overcoming your addiction will greatly improve your life. You should care enough about yourself to seek help in overcoming your addiction.

SLEEP

Sleep is a very important part of living a healthy and happy lifestyle, second only to eating a nutritious diet. Getting enough sleep every night can greatly improve your mood and well being (Digdon, Buro & Sheptycki, 2008). This Sleep allows your body and mind time to repair and energize itself for the next day. Sleep affects the following in your body:

- immune system
- metabolism
- hormones
- growth
- nervous system
- muscular system
- skeletal system
- memory
- mood
- cognitive function

There is a strong correlation between sleep and all of these functions. The more that your body is deprived of sleep, the more negatively these functions are affected.

One of the first questions you should ask yourself is whether you are getting enough sleep. The amount of sleep you need can be discovered by examining how you feel during the day having slept for different amounts of time the night before. Some people need only six hours of sleep, while others need ten. Most people fall into the seven- to eight-hour range.

How do you feel when you wake up and throughout your day? When you feel your best, how many hours of sleep have you slept the night before? These are all questions only you can answer. Everyone is different. If you are sleepy during the day or lacking energy, it could be because you are not getting enough sleep. It is also important that you have a good sleeping environment with comfortable bedding. This is easy to overlook, but how productive are you really going to be with horrible back or neck pain?

The LOA is all about living your life to the best of your ability. If more sleep is what you want from the universe, then ask for more hours. How much more time do you think you need? Thirty minutes? Two hours? Decide on how many hours will make keep you at your peak and feeling your best throughout the day and ask the universe to give you that many hours of sleep every night.

Perhaps you want better-quality sleep. Many people are in bed for eight hours but only asleep for part of that time or spend much of the night tossing and turning. This is not quality sleep, and it can have a negative impact on your day. You can use the LOA to help you attract a full night of quality sleep. You can ask the Universe for eight hours straight of sleep without waking up, if that is what you would like. Remember to ask for what you want and then allow it to happen.

Insomnia is defined as difficulty falling asleep or maintaining sleep, or both. According to the U.S. Department of Health and Human Services, it was estimated that in 2007, twenty percent of Americans suffered from insomnia. There are many causes of insomnia, but the LOA can help to eliminate these causes so that you are able to get a good night sleep, every night.

TIME MANAGEMENT

Effective time management also contributes to a healthy lifestyle. Effectively managing your time can improve your quality of life. The following are all benefits of time management:

- Reduced frustration
- More energy
- Puts you in control
- Productivity
- Increased satisfaction
- Increased quality/leisure time
- Creates piece of mind
- Easier to meet goals
- Boosts confidence

Time management encompasses your daily routine, short-term goals, and long-term goals. It includes organizing, planning, scheduling, prioritizing, delegating, setting goals, monitoring, and analysis. There is no specific method of time management. Proper time management includes all aspects of your life and your responsibilities, so everyone's execution of time management will be different. We are willing to bet that you lead a hectic life—most of us do. Between work, family, leisure time, activities, and chores, it could be possible to fill a thirty-hour day. In reality, you have about sixteen hours in your day if you plan on getting eight hours of sleep. Everyone feels crunched for time, no matter how busy they are.

Perhaps you wish to improve your time-management skills. You can attract better time management with the LOA. You can be organized and efficient in running your household and running your life. The key to time management is thinking ahead. One of the biggest frustrations of not managing time to the best of your ability is experiencing frustration of not doing something sooner. This often happens when it is too late or you are past a deadline on something. People tend to focus on the past and get mad at themselves for not having paid attention to the task earlier. This creates negative energy and will only serve to bring more procrastination into your life.

It is important to think and plan ahead of time so that you are able to complete tasks calmly and at your own pace instead of feeling rushed. Frustration usually occurs when you realize that you cannot get back time that has already passed. This is when panic sets in for many people who procrastinate. Your life does not have to be this way. Managing your time and future plans and obligations can reduce stress. The following affirmation can be used if you are a procrastinator. Eliminating procrastination will allow the LOA to work for you by helping you create a more organized and efficient schedule for your life and by reducing negativity that accompanies the stress that is created by poor time management.

> I now focus on my goal. The one goal I want to achieve. I now release all feelings of anxiety, fear of failure, and fear of success. I now release all of these feelings and relax. As I relax, I picture myself having accomplished my goal. I see myself there with the net result, having accomplished my goal, having completed my goal. I realize how powerful I am, and I will now allow myself to move forward and complete my goal. I realize how good I will feel once I have taken action toward completing my goal, once I have taken that first powerful step. I am very confident. I understand that I have the power

within myself, the focus and control within myself, to accomplish this goal. I now focus on the steps required to achieve this goal, and I see them all laid out in front of me in a timeline, leading me to my goal. And I now imagine myself above this timeline, toward the end, when I have achieved my goal. I look back at all the steps, and I realize that they are all very logical and I realize that I will allow those steps to happen. I relax as I look back from my goal, at those steps. I see them dating all the way back to the present time and I realize how easy it is and how logical it is to achieve my goal. And as I now float over this timeline, back to the present, I look to the future and I see all of the steps required to achieve my goal. And I realize that I have the inner resources to achieve my goal easily and powerfully and I realize that I will schedule each of these steps in a very logical manner and I am highly motivated to achieve my goal easily and confidently. I have all the resources I need to achieve my goal and I give myself permission, permission to achieve my goal.

There are varying degrees of procrastination. For some people, procrastination plagues their entire life and they cannot seem to ever truly be rid of it. This is also what happens when the LOA works against you. Procrastination tends to have a domino effect, causing a negative impact in all areas of your life—from simple daily chores to major life decisions. Realize that you can obtain complete control of your procrastination. You can use the LOA to attract efficient time management. Remember, focusing on procrastination will only bring you more procrastination in your life. Focusing on the positive—better and more effective time management—will help you attract the planning skills you need to better manage your life both in the short-term and the long-term.

If you feel that your time management or organizational skills could be improved, we encourage you to ask the universe to grant you the necessary skills so that you can effectively manage your life. Time management is more than just fitting everything you need to accomplish into your day. Lifestyle management is about organizing your life, which includes yourself, family, home, work, and your finances.

We often wish to create balance and inner peace within ourselves. This means asking the universe for peace and serenity. This line of thinking goes along with what we have been discussing throughout this book. *You* control your thoughts, actions, and emotions. When you feel you have control over these aspects of your life, you begin to think more positively and calmly, and serenity naturally comes into your life.

Managing your family is a major part of managing your lifestyle. No matter what your personal situation is—married or not, kids or no kids, or whether you have parents and siblings in your life—family is a major part of most people's lives. Managing your relationships with family members can sometimes be a challenge. For example, if you have a teenager, you know how challenging being a parent can be and how it can sometimes cause you to question your parenting. The LOA can give you more confidence in yourself and give you patience in the most difficult situations—you just have to ask for it. Another example might be having a strained relationship with a family member. Whether you choose to mend the relationship or not, you must choose to be at peace with your decision, and this often involves forgiveness. Forgiveness can give you peace of mind. Below is an affirmation you can use to help you forgive someone in your life:

> I realize just how wonderful I am. I am a wonderful, amazing person. I have immense integrity. I respect myself and others. And because I respect others, I allow myself now to forgive that person I need to forgive. I imagine that person right now, the person I desire to forgive. I realize that I do indeed desire to forgive him. He is human and I am human, and sometimes humans make mistakes. I accept this, realizing that I, just like everyone else, am capable at times of doing things that need to be forgiven. And as a wonderful, warm, caring person, I now make the decision to forgive that person. I have made the permanent decision to forgive him and to allow him back into my trust because I realize now that he is worthy of being forgiven. I reflect for a moment on all the wonderful things about him, all the wonderful things that make him unique. I realize that I will forgive him and I am very comfortable with this decision. I am very determined to forgive him, so I allow myself to let go of those feelings that I have been holding on to. I let go of those negative feelings now, those negative feelings concerning that person, I let go of them. I feel them leaving me now, those negative feelings are leaving me; they are being replaced by warm, wonderful, loving feelings toward that person. Day by day, I will decide to let this warm, wonderful feeling to increase.

When living with other people, it is natural to sometimes have to struggle to find balance. Oftentimes we do not seek balance, and instead we lead crazy and hectic lives. This leads to stress and can have a negative impact on our lives. The LOA sees this negative energy and gives back more chaos into your life. We encourage you to ask for balance in your family life so that every member in your household is happy and feels balanced. The LOA can reward you with effective time management and balance, making you feel more in control of managing your family life.

The third part of lifestyle and time management is your home life. Being organized at home can save tremendous worry, stress, and time. Clutter and disorganization in your household can lead to frustration, misplaced items, loss of important items, and chaos in general. It is important that you feel a sense of organization in your living space because this will lead to other good and positive feelings for the universe. Living in a messy home leads to wasted time trying to find things. The universe takes note of the frantic energy you give off when you live this way. You do not want this! You can take control of your clutter using the LOA. Just cleaning up your home slowly and over time will give you a sense of accomplishment, and the universe will reward you with organization.

Work is another major part of your life that demands time management and organization. It is important to keep your professional life and your personal life separate when that is possible. When you are at work, your focus should be on the tasks you need to accomplish and not on personal issues. We encourage you to take a good look at your job and ask yourself if you are managing your time to the best of your ability. Not managing your time at your job can be dangerous because it can lead to you getting fired or not being productive. The more productive you are, the better results you will see in your life with the LOA. Take pride in your work—this is very important. When you take pride in your work, you feel like a success and this creates positive energy.

Last, we have finances. We have already talked about wealth on a larger scale in your life. However, from a day-to-day perspective, your finances require budgeting and knowing how much money is coming in and going out. Keeping track of your finances puts you in charge and gives you a sense of control. When creating a budget or looking closely at your finances, it is important to maintain a positive attitude even if things look grim. Having a positive outlook on your finances will give you a more positive outlook on life. Staying organized and on top of bills will help you build wealth with the LOA. Ask the universe to give you control of your finances. You will be glad you did!

LEISURE

We all want to incorporate leisure time into our lifestyle. The good news is that the LOA can help you do so! Leisure time is time in which you can forget about all responsibilities and commitments and focus on something you enjoy doing. We all strive to have leisure time in our lives. What we decide to spend our leisure time doing can vary from person to person.

You probably have a hobby or several hobbies that you enjoy. A hobby is something you enjoy doing in your spare time. Usually personal fulfillment is the goal of having a hobby. Perhaps you like spending time outdoors, crafts, participating in team sports, playing video games, reading, or gardening. You are probably well aware of what you enjoy doing in your spare time. You might want to consider asking the universe for more leisure time so that you can focus more of your time on your hobby.

Using the LOA, you will want to ask for leisure time, if that is what you want from the universe. It may be helpful to remember that leisure time comes after you have accomplished important things in your life. Leisure time will only be granted to you if you deserve it and if you ask for it and allow it to enter your life. Many people have the time for leisurely activities, but they choose not to partake in them because they get more fulfillment from career or other pursuits. Leisure time allows you to relax and spend time enjoying yourself, so we suggest that you ask the universe for leisure time in your life. Many of us lead hectic and stressful lives. Leisure time is mandatory to allow our minds and bodies to rest, relax and recuperate from a busy and stressful lifestyle. For example, heart disease is the number one cause of death in the United States (Centers for Disease Control & Prevention, 2009). Leading a stressful life contributes to heart disease. As a result and for your own well-being, we suggest that you relax and take time for yourself—not only to improve your physical health, but your mental health as well.

A lot of people ask the universe for leisure time because they may want to take a vacation. Vacations are something that almost everyone looks forward to, but they also cannot always happen due to time and financial constraints. If you wish to make vacation time fit into your lifestyle, then we suggest you ask the universe for a vacation—it is that easy! Ask the universe for what you want, allow it into your life, and you will receive what you want. The fun thing about asking for a vacation from the universe is visualization! You can imagine yourself in your ideal vacation spot several times a day, which will help you ask for and allow yourself to be rewarded with vacation time.

19

Overview of What You Want and How to Get It

So far, we have addressed what people typically want to achieve in their lives and how to use the LOA to get it. While reading through our suggestions, you now feel very positive and hopeful that change will be possible for you in any or all of these categories through the LOA. Indeed, this is the case.

On paper, these categories may seem fairly mundane. However, let us not forget that when issues that we do not want to manifest in our lives do so, they can become huge obstacles that appear on the surface to be difficult or sometimes even impossible to overcome.

The categories we are referring to and have been focusing on are as follows:

Chapter 09—Abundance

Chapter 10—Happiness

Chapter 11—Health

Chapter 12—Wealth

Chapter 13—Relationships

Chapter 14—Relief from Stress

Chapter 15—Success

Chapter 16—Career

Chapter 17—Things

Chapter 18—Lifestyle

These ten categories, as innocuous as they may seem, cause the greatest suffering for people around the world when individuals feel they cannot have what they desire or things are not going the way that they want them to. In fact, these areas of life have caused inner turmoil and frustration in many people's lives for centuries. However, many people have also effectively used the LOA to rework all of these categories to their benefit. Countless people have been able to utilize the LOA to get what they want, and there is no reason that you cannot also achieve what you want in an easy and simple manner.

At first, the number of different methods and techniques described in the past chapters may seem a bit overwhelming. Often when people first get a taste of everything the LOA can bring them, they tend to feel intimidated. However, we are going to make this as easy as possible for you. The first step is for you to decide what you want in order to bring the powers of the LOA into your life. Your answer may be that you want "all of the above." It is actually quite common to not know which direction to proceed in first. The LOA is the golden ticket which can bring you what you want (and previously have only dreamed of), but which part of the ticket should you cash in first?

In previous chapters, we have overviewed exercises, affirmations, suggestions, and activities to emphasize attracting different elements. We will take a moment now to recap some of the highlights we have discussed. You can use this summary as a guide to remind you of which categories you want to improve in your life first. While reading the summaries of these areas of potential improvement, use your intuition to recognize which areas you want to focus on primarily. It may also be likely that you feel you have already reached success and balance in one or more of these areas. If that is the case, that is great news and you are already well on your way to achieving all that you want. Make sure that you maintain what you are currently doing in the areas of your life in which you are already happy.

ABUNDANCE

Abundance is the sense of fullness and the feeling of being complete. If you are experiencing abundance, it means that you are satisfied with all aspects of your life. Once you have decided that you want abundance in your life, the next step is to ask the universe for this abundance you are seeking.

In Chapter 9, we presented a metaphoric exercise that we suggested incorporating into your schedule if you are seeking abundance. Steve uses the exercise of a plant growing into a tree to assist in creating abundance and confidence in people. Though this technique is used in Steve's hypnosis practice, you can use this script yourself to bring change and results into your life even if you are not working directly with a hypnotist,

HAPPINESS

Happiness is different from abundance, as you can feel filled with deep happiness and still have very little. There are a variety of exercises and methods of thinking that can create more happiness in your life. The more happiness you cultivate, the more you will receive. This alone is a satisfactory reason to create and ask for more happiness in your life. In Chapter 10, some of the methods we discussed that are intended to create more happiness in your life included the following:

- Exercising
- Visualizing happiness using two pyramids
- Keeping a "gratitude journal"
- Meditation or prayer

The above four exercises are only a few of the many techniques that can easily bring more happiness into your life. If you are seeking happiness, focus on these powerful exercises and you will certainly begin to see your feelings of happiness flourish.

The principles behind happiness are similar to the ancient laws of karma that are known worldwide—"If you do good things, good things will happen to you; if you do bad things, bad things will happen to you." Similarly, if you think happy thoughts, happy things will come back to you.

HEALTH

For many people, the main point of focus in using the LOA would be their health. It is common that health stands out as many people's primary consideration. After all, if you do not have your health, all of your other intentions and material desires may seem inconsequential. Achieving success, relationships, wealth, etc. may seem all of a sudden far less important if you do not have a healthy body with which to achieve these goals.

In Chapter 11, we focused on a sample script that Steve uses with his hypnotherapy patients who seek improved health. This script focuses on a green cleansing liquid that is poured into our body that cleanses and purifies our bodies, bringing us to optimal health. We have found this script to be very helpful in bringing a healthier lifestyle to a wide variety of people, and we encourage you to try it.

WEALTH

Many people begin using the LOA as a method by which to attain wealth. One important factor that many overlook is that it is hugely important to decide and become very specific about how much money you want, and when you want it to arrive by. As we discussed in Chapter 12, in order to attract wealth into your life, it is important to feel as financially abundant as possible. We suggested some effective visualization exercises, such as keeping a $100 bill in your pocket, and when you see something that you like for $100, go through the mental process of what it is like to buy that item. This experience fosters a sense of financial prosperity. Also, creating a wealth box to fill with anything and everything that represents wealth to you is an important step in the process of visualizing what you want. It is very important that you believe that you will receive the things that you want. Another suggestion is to listen to or practice unlimited wealth self-hypnosis.

RELATIONSHIPS

Whether it is a romantic relationship or friends that you seek, keep focused on the qualities that you want to find in your relationships, as we described in Chapter 13. Imagine exactly what you are looking for in a friend or romantic relationship using as detailed imagery as you can. Once you have identified what you want and ask the universe for it, simply visualize it, ask for it, allow it to happen and then receive it.

RELIEF FROM STRESS

You will find that once you begin changing your negative thoughts into positive ones, your stress will begin to evaporate. Usually stress is the result of our thinking and emotions that have been negative. It may also be a result of past occurrences that have left you feeling overwhelmed.

The trick to taking care of stress is to start using the LOA to draw more positivity into your life as well as actively make changes to become more positive and reduce your stress. Think through the factors or aspects of your life that are stressful to you, and actively participate in using the LOA to release these factors. One great exercise that will assist you in doing so is outlined in Chapter 14 and consists of making a list each morning with three columns. The first column should include things that are important to accomplish, the second column will include the reasons why, and then the third column will contain an estimate of how long each item takes. Completing this exercise will serve to provide relief from stress, and an added benefit is that by doing it often enough, it will become automatic to some degree, leaving you having to spend even less time focusing on reducing stress in your life and instead living a more stress free life.

SUCCESS

Success does not have any particular designation of importance. This is because your gauge for whether you have achieved success in your life should be based on whether you genuinely feel successful. Many people are actually afraid of achieving success in their ventures and this fear sometimes serves to only hold people back from achieving success.

In Chapter 15, we discuss the notion that fear of success is often based on fear of the unknown, which is an intrinsic characteristic of human nature. Figuring out what you want and what will make you be successful in this world is one of the keys to letting go of fear of success.

Some other key points discussed in Chapter 15 include:

- Do not give up! Keep asking the LOA for what you want.
- Change your mindset to focus on the positive. Do not focus on past events as failures, but instead focus on what is ahead for you, in the future.
- Above all, remember: you define what success is for you. Do not fall into the painful trap of letting others determine what success is for you—not your family, especially not your friends and not

society. You determine what you want and what will make you happy, and no one else—ever.

CAREER

The LOA can be effectively utilized under many circumstances—whether you are happy with your career and want to maintain it, whether you are happy with parts of your career and not others, or whether you need to change your career completely to something you enjoy more—the steps can and will help.

Visualization is a highly effective tool that can help you identify the ideal career you wish to pursue or simply bring more satisfying results to your current career. In Chapter 16, we included a sample script that Steve uses with people who are looking to figure out their ideal careers. If you find yourself in that situation, make a note of this script and read thought it. This script is very powerful at helping you zero in on your perfect job. Once you have identified it, take the appropriate actions to make it a reality, and use the exercises we have shared with you to effectively use the LOA to bring it to you.

THINGS

Specific things that you want in your life can be brought to you by the same means as the other areas. You must visualize what it is that you want, ask for it, allow it to enter your life, receive it, and then be thankful for it.

To use the LOA in attracting things that you want into your life, we suggested writing a list of the things that you really want but do not have yet. Carry this list around with you and place it where you will see it as much as possible. View the things on this list as things that you will have soon. Your focus should be on how they will contribute to your overall happiness.

In Chapter 17, we discussed specific visualizations you can use to attract the things you may want into your life. We overviewed visualizations on getting a house, a car, and other nice things that we may want delivered into our lives through the LOA.

LIFESTYLE

Your lifestyle choices have an unequivocal impact on everything else in your life. Chapter 18 focused on the types of lifestyle changes we can make to benefit ourselves in a holistic, all-encompassing way.

The first focus is healthy eating and exercise. Chapter 18 offers sample affirmations that you can use to help you change your focus to view food as a fuel that will make and keep you healthier. We also included a sample affirmation that Steve recommends and uses to help clients attract the love of exercise into their lives. Scripts that assist with quitting habits such as smoking or other addictions were also included in this chapter and are also important to use, as these issues are mandatory to get help with in order to make the LOA work for you.

Sleep and time management are also addressed in this chapter. The LOA can help you achieve better time management skills. Planning ahead and releasing tendencies to procrastinate are integral in reducing stress and managing your time effectively. Finding leisure time is also key and mandatory toward keeping our bodies and minds running smoothly.

MAKING YOUR BEST CHOICES DAY TO DAY

This recap of past chapters should be helpful in refreshing your memory and helping you prioritize in which areas of your life you want or need to work on first. Take as much time as you need to review the past chapters and undoubtedly, one or two areas will stand out as being most important to you at this point in time in your life.

Of course, the LOA also includes positive actions in all areas. When living in conjunction with the principles of the LOA, it is necessary to promote and obtain balance in our lives and harmony in all areas of our existence. One obvious area to concentrate on and be cognizant of at all times would be health. After all, without feeling good and being in a state of good health, all of our other dreams may fall by the wayside. If we want to rid ourselves of disease and achieve optimal health in general, it is a good idea to practice all of the activities and actions that we know improve health. For example, include a variety of fruits and vegetables in your diet, and develop an exercise routine that consists of something you enjoy doing.

Science is making progress at the speed of light in almost every field, and each year that goes by progress becomes faster. Scientific progress is also evident in the fields of medicine and nutrition. There is now no excuse for not knowing that certain foods are your friend and others, like processed foods, are not nutritious to consume.

Numerous scientific studies have shown that a positive mental attitude can actually boost our immune system (Kotz, 2006 & Veenhoven et al., 2008). Creating and having a strong immune system means that your body will not only fight off diseases, viruses, and bacteria more effectively, it can even tackle diseases such as cancer with more vigor and success. Something as simple as laughing has also been proven to boost the immune system. We now know that there really *is* something to the old saying, "Laughter is the best medicine." The great news is that along with taking other steps to improve your health and reduce stress, whatever you can do that will make you laugh, make you happy or make you more relaxed will actually help your body and health by improving your immune system.

Keeping healthy is vital to achieving your goals. A large part of good health that is often overlooked is keeping your stress level low. While it may sound obvious, you cannot achieve your dreams if you are seriously ill or dead. This is why tackling stress is so critical to your long-term success.

Thinking positive thoughts and experiencing positive emotions will not be nearly as effective if you are smoking, drinking, and doing drugs. Again, balance in all parts of your life is important to making good things happen and the LOA work for you.

A great way to relieve stress is by getting enough sleep. Once again, sleep is overlooked as an important element of health by many, but it's critical for our overall functioning. Think about it: would evolution really shut us down for about thirty-three percent of the time for no reason? Biologists will tell you that nature doesn't waste resources. That is not how evolution works. If sleep weren't necessary, nature would have dictated that humans would not sleep so that they could be out foraging for food, for example. Sleep helps combat stress and heals our bodies and minds.

The bottom line is that what relieves stress varies from person to person. What may be stressful for one person may provide stress relief for another. Ask yourself what truly relieves stress for you. Do not just go along with society's definition of stress relief, although there are techniques that generally work for many people that you may want to try, such as yoga, spending time around nature, and exercising. However, one person's way to de-stress will not necessarily be another's. If you believe most movies are junk and feel stressed out when you go to the movies, then don't go. If you feel that snowboarding is stressful, don't do it. You get the idea. Like so many things in life, the trick is to determine what is best for you and what works for you, and so long as it does not harm anyone else, go for it.

We also reviewed relationships in Chapter 13. When choosing your relationships, strive to make sure that those relationships will not interfere with your goals. Befriending or associating with individuals that do not value you as a person or show you respect or kindness will not lead to happiness in the long run. Ask yourself if the people with whom you have surrounded yourself with are trustworthy people that have your best interest at heart. Remember to be honest with yourself about the answer. It is sad to say, but the world is full of people who take pleasure in seeing other people fail. They inaccurately believe that there exists a limited amount of resources and wealth in the universe and that your success might be at their expense. A well-placed saboteur can do incalculable damage to your goals.

DECIDING WHAT YOU WANT

It can often be the case that when people begin working with the LOA, they feel intimidated by the vast range of things that they desire. At that point, it can become confusing to know what areas to focus on first. It is common to be hesitant to prioritize one area over another in your life. So how do you make a decision on which path to proceed on first? The LOA is, at its essence, about positive feelings, so the answer to this question is simply that you must look in the direction of what area makes you happiest and fosters the most enthusiasm in your core.

If you want to bring all of these areas into your life, that is fine. Go ahead! Similarly, if you feel that you only have the focus to concentrate on one very small area to begin with, that is also a fine way to proceed. You know on a subconscious level what is right for you, so use your intuition when getting started and trust yourself. If you feel in any way overwhelmed by the limitless possibilities of the LOA, we suggest picking out one or two of the scripts that we have provided in this book and one daily LOA exercise to start. This is not mandatory, but rather just a suggestion. If you might want to incorporate every single exercise at first, then go right ahead! There are no set rules on how to begin. When using the LOA, you make the rules, and you should feel free to change them at your leisure.

ASK FOR ALL THAT YOU WANT

In the early 1900s, Wallace Wattles wrote a book about the LOA entitled *The Science of Getting Rich.* In his book, Wattles wrote about a very poor man who used the LOA to bring things into his life. The things he had asked the universe for were meagre; and he then found that he had not asked for enough.

> I recall now the case of one student who was told that he must get in mind a clear picture of what he desired so that the creative thought of them could be impressed on formless substance. He was a very poor man, lived in a rented house, and having had only what he earned from day to day, he could not grasp that all wealth was his. So, after thinking the matter over, he decided that he might reasonably ask for a new rug for the floor of his best room, and a coal stove to heat the house during the cold weather. Following the instructions given in this book, he obtained these things in just a few months. Then it dawned on him that he had not asked for enough.

Similarly to this man who initially did not ask for enough, if you find yourself just seeking a meager portion of what you truly want in the beginning of your practice of the LOA, those will be the results that you receive. You may later on end up wishing that you had asked for more. It is up to you to dream big, visualize your greatest visions, and accept the rewards. You should not feel pressured or hindered to ask for a small segment of what you want. Doing so is often based on potentially negative past thoughts or beliefs.

Your past programming may try to tell you that it is impossible to get everything that you want now and that it is necessary to prioritize your goals. If that is essential for you as a chosen path, then you can proceed in this manner. However, if you want to get everything you want now, realize that this is also within your reach. It is up to you to ask for the biggest things, and accept the universe's largest gifts.

The LOA works in conjunction with and in fact is dependent upon our thoughts and emotions. When we react to life in a positive manner, the universe takes notice and brings more positive elements into your life—including your health. If you are thinking and experience positive emotions, you will find that the universe is also offering you radiance and perfect health.

20

Step Four: Ask for It

It is necessary to take this following step in order to get what you want. We have just talked about the steps you need to take before you ask for what you want. The reason for doing this is so that you know what you do want and you realize how important it is to focus on the positive and the future rather than the negative and the past.

Asking for what you want may seem like a very simple step, and it is; but for some people, it can be a bit of a challenge. During hypnosis, a hypnotherapist can program people to ask for what they want, but you can program yourself by making the decision that you will ask for whatever it is you want. While you are envisioning what you want, go ahead and ask for it every day until you receive it. Perhaps every morning when you wake up or every night before you go to bed you will ask the universe for whatever it is that you want. Go ahead and say, "Universe, I want _____."

In the previous steps, we outlined the different things you may want to ask the universe for. In addition, we gave you examples about how to incorporate these things into your life. We gave examples such as visualizations, attraction and wealth boards and boxes, making lists, and leaving notes in various places to serve as reminders. All of these things are ways in which you ask the universe for what you want. The combination of all of these examples will help you move toward your goal with the LOA. However, the most powerful thing you can do is to directly ask the universe for what you want. Do so every single day.

THE POWER OF ASKING

We have repeatedly stated throughout this book that you have to ask for what you want—this is the first positive action you are preparing. It is as simple as that. It is a simple step, but a step that must be repeated day after day until you receive what you are asking for. The entire time that you are asking for what you want to receive, you must also truly believe that eventually you will receive it. Think back to Step One and how we were preparing you to keep a positive outlook—this is where it comes in handy. We do not want you to feel frustrated if after a week, month, year, or ten years, your dream has not manifested. Keeping faith in the LOA is mandatory throughout this process.

You must know what you want. You may have already decided on what you wish to manifest in your life using the LOA. There may be many different areas of your life that you want to change. You have considered all of these areas and you have decided on what you want. Only when you fully want something and ask for it everyday can you move on to the next step.

INTENTIONS

Intentions are an often overlooked source of energy that can be extremely important and powerful. Consider that energy is the universe itself; it is all around us and ready for the taking whenever you want and need it. Your emotions are actually the result of energy, and they are extremely powerful when focused on your intentions.

Both intentions and emotions are key components in getting what you want out of life. Intentions describe the emotional focus of asking for what you want, as mentioned in Step Three of the LOA process. There are several things you may be wondering about right now. How do your emotions affect your intentions? Are your emotions directly aligned with your intentions? We can tell you that if they are not, it is a safe bet that you can expect not to attract your vision.

Though your emotions must be aligned with your intentions, this is not always natural for many people. However, not to worry—you have complete control over both, and we are going to explain how this is so. Making sure your intentions are constantly aligned with your emotions is one of the most-overlooked steps of the LOA process. At the beginning of this book, we discussed why your emotions and your thoughts are so important in the LOA, but we are revisiting it here so that you may realize the importance of frequently reassessing your intentions every step of the way.

What sometimes happens is that someone consciously puts out an intention, and when he does not receive the results he was hoping for, he immediately assumes that it is the LOA that does not work. We are here to tell you that the LOA does exist—and it works every time. However, your intentions must be emotionally charged and true. If you follow the principles we have outlined here and throughout the rest of this book, you too can experience the power of the LOA. However, this is such a key component that we must repeat—throughout the entire process, your intentions and your emotions must be in alignment with the LOA in order to make it work for you.

Your intentions are your purpose. Your purpose is right now to allow the LOA to work in your life. If you want the LOA to work for you, then your intentions have to be in alignment with your purpose. You have the ability to attract *anything*. All you have to do is follow the six steps outlined in this book, exclude negative thoughts from your mind, keep your intentions focused on your dream, and most important, eliminate all the negative influences in your life. This can be a challenging step, but remember that negative people equal negative energy, and surrounding yourself with negative influences will be all you need to experience no success with the LOA. You have the power to be, do, and achieve anything you want using these principles. It is all there for you to experience, enjoy and take advantage of, if you know how to. We are teaching you how you can attract anything you want into your life. We hope that at this point in time in the book, you are excited and full of hope about manifesting your dreams with the Law of Attraction.

Now that you have learned just how important and powerful your intentions actually are, it is time to ask yourself and examine just what your intentions really are. The time has also come to truly decide if your emotions are aligned with these same intentions. The first sign that your emotions may not be aligned with your intentions is when you are not getting what you want. If this is the case, now is the time to take a step back and analyze your intentions, which include your thoughts and emotions. You need to review exactly what it is within the universe that is stopping you from getting what you really want. It can be a number of interferences that may include your emotions, intentions, lack of focus, and the potential negative energy that may be surrounding you and therefore representing negative energy in your thoughts as well.

Your thoughts are very powerful, and they literally put out a frequency into the universe. This frequency is very commanding, and ideally you want to use this for your benefit—using the universe to deliver what it is you want through these thoughts and frequencies. It is important to understand that if one step is missing out of this process or if the frequencies you are giving off are not 100 percent pure and accurate, you are not going to get what you want from the universe. This may sound overwhelming at first, but the process is attainable and made easier when you take the time to really work at it and perfect it. You must be clear and already know what it is you want to manifest for yourself and your expectations because it is often the case that the universe has already sent you something, but you may not even realize it.

You may be wondering now if the universe has already delivered something to you that you wanted or if it is possible that you may have already attracted what you really wanted and perhaps didn't realize it. It is important to be clear on the correct answers to these questions so that you can become more aware of the universe and what you experience in your life. For example, if the universe gives you something you have been trying to attract, check it off your list—either your physical list or the list in your mind.

This is something that has happened time and time again, even to the authors. There have been many occasions on which we have thought that one of our intentions did not manifest, but upon taking a closer look at our lives, we found that the universe did provide this intention for us, albeit in a form we failed to recognize at first.

What can easily happen when you think you have not attracted a certain intention into your life is that you become full of negative emotions and thoughts. These thoughts can then further inhibit your intentions and emotions, causing them to become aligned negatively and this powerful (negative) frequency is what you wind up giving off. It is important to keep in mind that grasping the concept of the LOA is not something that happens overnight. It can take weeks, months, or years to manifest your dreams. Prepare yourself to have patience. More important than this, understand that it takes time to practice and utilize each and every step and tool properly throughout many different life situations.

Making sure that everything works together in balance and harmony is the key to utilizing the LOA properly. If one step of this process is flawed ever so slightly, the rest of the process will not work either. On the other hand, if the entire process is practiced properly, the universe is then going to provide you with exactly what you want.

We hope that you have learned the importance of asking clearly for what you want. Asking for what you want is more complicated than it may seem at first glance, but have faith that you will realize the importance of asking the universe for the things you want out of life. Be a deliberate creator of your life. You are the only person who has control over what you ask for and receive from the universe. Everything that exists is a creation of our thoughts. Asking for what you want will help make your dreams a reality.

You may be wondering how asking for what you want could be so powerful. Asking for what you want means you are focusing on what you want. Concentration and focus on the things you want in life give energy to those things. When you give positive energy to the things that you want to add to your life, the universe takes notice and rewards you with more positive energy, and soon, you receive the things you have been asking the universe to deliver to you.

Remember, everything you think, feel, and act upon creates energy. Your goal is to have the energy that you give off be positive, because positive energy is more powerful than you can comprehend—it is truly limitless, just as the universe is. When you ask for what you want every day and give off positive energy, you are creating powerful vibrations that the universe has to pay attention to. The LOA is very powerful.

Every day, strive to physically, mentally, and spiritually put yourself in a positive and empowered state of mind and ask the universe for the things you want. It is that simple. You can master the art of putting yourself in a state of joy. This state will encourage positive energy for when you ask the universe for whatever it is that you want.

21

Step Five: Allow It

The next step in the LOA process is to allow it. This simply means that whatever it is that you are asking for you have to allow into your life. The key during this step is to truly ask yourself if you are allowing yourself to attract whatever it is that you are trying to attract. There is a big difference between *saying* that you are allowing something into your life and *thinking and feeling* with your entire being that you are allowing it in. All three of these actions—thinking, feeling, and allowing great things into your life—have to be in alignment for the LOA to work for you. There is nothing too big that you can ask for.

Some people may find when implementing Step Five that they may not be willing to allow the things they want into their lives because they may feel as though they do not deserve it. This is not true. Everyone deserves all the good things in life. You deserve to be happy. You deserve to be in a fantastic relationship that you find fulfilling. You deserve to be in an optimal state of health. You deserve to be in the best possible career you can be in. You deserve to be wealthy. You must keep reminding yourself that you deserve all of these great things in your life. You need to allow whatever miracles are going to come your way to come into your life. You need to open your door and allow for those miracles to come into your life.

While you are allowing the LOA to come into your life, you also need to make sure that the previous four steps are in place. As we have said before, you must follow each step before proceeding to the next step. There is no point in rushing through the process. Take your time with each of these steps. Allowing the LOA into your life will not happen if you have not mastered Step One, which is all about having a positive attitude and outlook on your future. Steps Two and Three are equally as important to master. Allowing things into your life cannot happen if you have not figured out what you do and do not want in life. Knowing what you want is empowering. Figuring out what you want out of life puts you that much closer to reaching your dreams. The Fourth Step—asking for what you want—is the next step to accomplish. Asking for what you want becomes much simpler when you have mastered the first three steps.

It will help to continually remind yourself to no longer focus on the things you do not want. Instead, concentrate as often as possible on the things you do want to attract into your life. As often as possible throughout the day and in many different ways, remind yourself and envision the things that you want. Make sure that you are always asking for these things, and remember to never lose sight of what you are looking for. Be open to receiving rewards for your positive thinking, emotions, and behavior. You deserve it and you will attract your vision! Allowing good things into your life can be a challenging step, but we are here to help you along with the process. Allowing the LOA to work for you in a positive way has a lot to do with self-acceptance and feeling worthy of wonderful things. We cannot stress how much you deserve to be happy. You deserve great things in your life.

Below is an exercise that we suggest reading, preferably in front of a mirror so that you can look at yourself while doing so. This exercise is meant to give you a boost in self-esteem so that you can allow abundance, on many different levels, into your life.

> I am realizing now just how powerful I am. I am a very powerful, amazing, wonderful person. I am standing in front of this mirror, looking at my reflection. I see myself in the reflection of this mirror. I am taking a good look at what I see. I notice how amazing I am. I notice how wonderful I am. I am very attractive. Day by day, I begin to notice these things more and more. I realize how smart and intelligent I am. I am a very smart, very successful, very motivated person. I look at myself now in this mirror and notice these things; these things are very obvious to me and everyone around me, everyone in my life, everyone I know, everyone I will know. They will all notice

these things, my happiness, how smart I am, and how successful I am.
I am a wonderful, positive, beautiful person. I will now imagine three
things about myself which make me unique and wonderful, three
things. Perhaps it is how kind I am, how big-hearted I am. Perhaps it
is my perseverance, my creativity. I am thinking of three things about
myself that make me wonderful and unique. It is easy for me to think
of these things now, and each time I do this exercise I can think of
three new things that make me wonderful and unique. I know that
these things are not a secret; everyone knows how great I am. I am
taking a deep breath in now and breathing in the sense of abundance
that comes with being a wonderful person. As I exhale slowly, I let go
of any negative thoughts; they are no longer a part of me. I continue
breathing easily, effortlessly, and comfortably. Day by day I allow the
LOA to work for me, more and more. I realize that I am a very powerful, wonderful, amazing, beautiful, intelligent, smart person. I am
empowered by the LOA. In fact, my ability to let good things into my
life is limitless. I am infinite in my ability to allow wonderful things
into my life. Day by day I will realize this and feel good about myself.
I am full of a powerful sense of love for myself. And I use this energy
to allow abundance into my life. I am kind to others and I am kind to
myself. I respect myself. I deserve honor and respect. So I will only
put myself in situations which honor myself and avoid negative situations. And this enhances my ability to allow great things into my life.
Every day I will look for something I can do for myself, something
wonderful that I can do for myself and I will do it. Something that
shows me how wonderful I am. I do this for myself because I honor
and respect myself and I treat myself right. I deserve and allow abundance into my life. I do all of these things because I respect myself. I
allow myself to engage in all of these positive, wonderful activities
because I respect myself. I have a wonderful, powerful sense of self-
esteem. I am a wonderful, amazing person.

OVERCOME FEAR OF SUCCESS

Step Five—allowing it—deals with the fear of success in relation
to the LOA. So many times we see people who have gone through the
first four steps, and the thing that they wanted will show up in one
way or another at their doorstep. Whether it is the person of their
dreams, the perfect job, the opportunity to travel, the opportunity to
write a book, the opportunity to be in a movie—eventually it will
show up in their lives (if they have believed in it). Step Five simply
says that you must allow it into your life. You must open that door and
let it in, and that is a very simple process if you look at it mechani-

cally. However, people can turn even the simplest concept into something complex by tapping into baggage they may have from their past. The fear of success has many negative implications in your life (Miller, 1994).

To illustrate this, imagine if the perfect mate shows up for you because you have asked for her, and then you somehow sabotage that relationship because at a subconscious level, you may not be allowing it to happen. This is what we mean by not allowing the LOA to work for you. Although you may say you want a relationship, you may also find a way to unravel that relationship because you have not properly prepared yourself on a subconscious level to truly receive that person and to allow her to actually be a part of your life. You are not allowing that person to be in your life even though she has shown up.

There are many different ways to sabotage a relationship, through such things as lying, cheating, losing interest, and causing arguments. These can undo a relationship and are often caused by your own subconscious mind fighting against you. Your subconscious mind does this because it does not actually want a relationship. This has to do with fear of success. The reason people sabotage a relationship is because they are fearful of being successful in a relationship. Unfortunately we also see this in many other areas of life.

People sometimes sabotage their chances at wealth because of their fear of success. The fear of being financially successful can cause you to do such things as overspend, get yourself into excessive debt, not pay your bills on time, and other actions which eventually undermine and eliminate wealth. When you have not properly prepared yourself to allow wealth into your life, you will find a way to get rid of that money because you are not comfortable with it. This all has to do with fear of success, and more specifically in this case, financial success. It is important for you to train yourself to accept success in your life.

The way that fear of success is treated in hypnotherapy is by reprogramming your mind to accept wealth, or in the case of a relationship, to accept the relationship. However, you can also do this in your everyday life by simply telling yourself that you are worthy of good things, initially making yourself accept the good things and identifying the sabotaging patterns when they arise.

We have identified ten main problems which fear of success can cause:

- Failing to achieve your full potential
- Feelings of guilt toward success

- Sabotaging your success
- Making inappropriate decisions about your future
- Belittling your own achievements
- Failing to follow through with visions you have set for yourself, which include financial and personal goals
- Self-destructive actions
- Inability to make decisions
- Inability to solve problems
- Lack of motivation to succeed

We realize that many of you have not yet experienced the LOA. It may take a long time, several re-evaluations, and a lot of changes in order to make the LOA work for you to the fullest potential. During the process you may come to realize many things you never knew about yourself. Perhaps you fear success in some form. You must find a way to overcome the fear of success so that you become willing to welcome great things in your life.

At first, it can be very hard for people to admit that they have a fear of success. They often claim that they want the LOA to work for them. The real truth is often that they do, but they are not fully ready for the success and abundance that the LOA brings. Their minds cannot truly make sense of this until they are able to overcome their fear of success.

People who fear success may feel that once they get what they want from the LOA, it may not be everything they were hoping it would be. They are often scared that they will not be as happy as they thought reaching their goals would make them. This is a very legitimate fear and, further, one that can really get in the way of reaching life goals. As you can see, it is essential to overcome the fear of success to make the LOA work for you.

You may be asking, "How do I overcome my fear of success?" You can overcome your fear of success the same way you accepted the LOA—by reinforcing your belief in yourself and in the universe. Start by realizing that you have many positive attributes and by reminding yourself that you have worked hard in life and you deserve to be rewarded. Many people find it helpful to remind themselves to praise something that they did each and every day.

Positive self-talk is also very helpful and it is highly advocated by us. It is important for you to be honest and open with yourself and to banish any negative outlook about your achievements. Positive self-talk promotes positive thinking, and it also helps you believe in yourself so that you will work even harder to achieve your goals. You can also incorporate self-talk into your visualizations. Remind yourself every day of how capable and accomplished you are.

Another great way to overcome the fear of success is to visualize your success. Most people are actually quite adept at this. Just as you visualize the things you want in life, you should add success with the LOA to what you envision. Imagine yourself successful and becoming abundant with the LOA. Imagine yourself happy, content, accomplished, and motivated. Visualize allowing great things to happen to you in your life! Remember, you have to ask for success and allow it into your life. Overcoming the fear of success is, at its core, all about believing in yourself.

Another tool that you may find helpful to use to overcome the fear of success are daily affirmations. Daily affirmations are statements that are repeated daily that inspire you to be the best you can be. They reaffirm all of your positive and fantastic attributes. We encourage you to find statements that inspire you—or you can try writing your own—whatever works best for you. Below are a few examples of positive-thinking affirmations used to overcome fear of success:

- I deserve to be successful.
- It is my destiny to be successful and to maintain and increase that success.
- I am worthy of all the good things life has to offer.
- I am successful in all areas of my life: mentally, physically, spiritually, financially, and emotionally.

Below is a variation of the success script that we have already included in this book in Chapter 15. However, we ask that when you read it this time, you try to think of it in a different way. We want you to think of it in relation to allowing the LOA into your life. You want to be successful at allowing anything and everything you want into your life, and this script will help you do just that.

> I realize that I am worthy of the Law of Attraction. I deserve to be successful. I see it. I feel it. I see, feel, and allow success into my life. I imagine myself successful. I notice what is surrounding me. I notice my environment. I see all the things I wish to attract with the Law of Attraction, and I am successful. I see how the Law of Attraction has changed my life. I see how others treat me and how I am respectful of others. I am a wonderful person and I deserve positive

things in my life. It feels so good to allow the Law of Attraction to work in all areas of my life, mentally, physically, spiritually, financially, and emotionally—in all of the areas in my life. I am successful. I see and feel myself being successful, and I realize that I will maintain and allow great things to enter my life. I will continue to be successful with the Law of Attraction because allowing good things into my life is a positive event for all of people in my life as well as myself. I set an example of how people should and can live and how they can reach their full potential, so my success benefits everyone in my life, because by seeing myself as a successful person, it helps others realize their own potential. By allowing the Law of Attraction to work for me, I benefit everyone in my life. I realize how much I deserve this. I deserve it 100 percent. I deserve to be happy, and as I breathe in deeply now, I breathe in strength and courage and as I exhale, I let go of fear. And as I breathe in, I breathe in worthiness. I am worthy of all the good things life has to offer. And as I exhale, I let go of all the rest of my fear, I let it go. I am a successful person, I feel the Law of Attraction entering my life. I feel it deep within me. I have always understood deep down inside that I deserve great things, and now I realize that it is absolutely true. It is my destiny to be positive and allow positive energy into my life and to maintain and increase success. So now I relax, and I realize that the Law of Attraction is working for me and I will continue to increase my success day by day by allowing more success into my life with the Law of Attraction. And I take those steps in a very powerful way because I deserve to be happy. I relax and realize just how successful I am and how much more successful I will become because I deserve to be successful with the Law of Attraction.

Once you have realized that you can reach for success, you must stay on this course. Be strong, and do not let others dissuade you in any way. You must also allow other people to compliment you and, for your part, believe what they say about you. Allow yourself to eliminate the negative feedback from those around you and only let in the good. You know the difference between positive and negative feedback. You can accept criticism by realizing that any kind of feedback allows you to grow as a person. Therefore, be willing to accept helpful criticism and realize that it ultimately contributes to your success. You will know when you have overcome your fear of success: You either will realize that you have achieved great success or you will be on the road to achieving great things. You will also know that you have reached success when you feel abundant. Abundance allows you to feel success even if you have not necessarily reached all of your goals.

The LOA is very powerful and with time, you will realize the true potential of attraction. When you receive what you have been asking for and you fully accept it into your life, then you have reached success.

THE POWER OF ALLOWING

Allowing good and positive energy into your life is a positive action that you must create room for in your life. The power of allowing is also known as the art of allowing. It is a skill and it is a skill you can master. Allowing good things to flow into your life takes practice and focus. You must truly feel as though you deserve good things to happen to you. You must let go of the negative aspects of your life in your past and only focus on the present and the future.

The process of attracting things into your life with the LOA cannot happen without the power of allowing. Allowing must occur on all levels, both consciously and subconsciously. You are probably already working on improving your conscious thoughts, which are the thoughts that go through your mind that you are aware of. These thoughts are easiest to control, but are not always *easy* to control. You have to become aware of them first, and then change them into positive thoughts instead of negative thoughts. The action of allowing is a positive action. Closing yourself off or preventing good things from happening in your life is a negative action. Consciously, you must strive to always be aware of all negative behaviors and thoughts and change them into positive actions, behaviors and thoughts of allowing.

Controlling your subconscious thoughts, feelings, and actions can be a bit trickier, however, as we are usually not aware of subconscious thoughts. However, it is important to be aware that subconscious thoughts could be keeping you from allowing the LOA into your life. The best method of accessing and controlling your subconscious mind is by using self-hypnosis. Self-hypnosis has been proven to provide many positive therapeutic benefits (Carmody & Baer, 2008). Later in this book, you will find that we will have an entire chapter dedicated to self-hypnosis and how it can help you with the LOA and allowing good things into your life. Self-hypnosis can help reprogram your subconscious mind so that you can make sure your subconscious thoughts and feelings are positive ones. It is entirely possible to gain control over your subconscious mind through self-hypnosis and since this will help you make progress using the LOA, we highly suggest trying it with an open mind.

What is so powerful about the LOA is that you have so many choices. Just like in life, certain choices will take you down certain roads. Using the LOA, you choose what you want to attract and what you do not want to attract. You must also choose to ask for things into your life and you must also choose to allow those things into your life. When you think about it, the past does not exist and neither does the future. All one can really know is the present. This means that you must always try to be in the present and focus on what you want right now and allow it to happen to you right now. It is only when you allow for good things to happen to you in the present that the universe delivers good things to you in the future. Asking for what you want in your life right now and allowing the things you want to occur in your life are things you must think about every day until you are able to move onto the next step: receiving.

As you can see, the art of allowing yourself to attract the things you want into your life can be somewhat challenging. You have to allow the LOA to work for you on many different levels: consciously, subconsciously, and through your thoughts, feelings, and actions. All of this has to happen simultaneously in order for you to effectively be allowing things into your life. Realize that you *can* do it! You create your own positive vibrations, and when you are truly allowing good things to happen to you, the universe will reward your positive energy with more wonderful things. Conversely, negative thoughts, feelings, and emotions do not create positive vibrations. By excessively worrying or doubting as to whether you are truly allowing the LOA to work for you, you may be cutting yourself off from attracting great things. It is very important that you believe in your ability to allow. You must want to allow good things into your life. You must feel as though you deserve great things. Not a single bone in your body can doubt your success with the LOA. We believe in you. We know you can accomplish great things by allowing the LOA into your life. You have to believe in yourself too!

BEING GRATEFUL FOR WHAT YOU ALREADY HAVE

Another important acknowledgment that should be made in relation to the art of allowing is the importance of being grateful for what you already have. When you are grateful for the goodness you already have in your life, you give off positive energy. The universe gives back this positive energy in various ways. We are assuming that if you look closely, there are many things in your life that are currently going well for you. It is important that you acknowledge all the good things that are present in your life right now. This is a powerful part of allowing the LOA to work for you.

We would like you to take a moment and think about the various parts of your life and truly ask yourself, what aspects are going well for me right now? What can I be grateful for? We suggest examining all aspects of your life. We have listed many factors below and we suggest going through each one while asking yourself if there is something in the category that you can be thankful for.

- Attitude
- Happiness
- Health
- Mood
- Energy
- Job
- Wealth
- Family
- Intimate relationship
- Friendship
- Inspiration
- Lifestyle
- Things
- Strength
- Home
- Relief from stress

You will notice that these are many of the things we talked about in Step Three while discussing what you can attract with the LOA. We are aware that you may already have some of these things going well for you in your life right now. It is important to think about each of them and realize what it is that you have. You may be happy with the job you have right now—and you should be thankful that you have a job. You can also think of the various aspects of your job that you enjoy and be thankful for those things. Perhaps you have a really close friend in your life who is very supportive of you—you should be thankful for her friendship. There are always things to be thankful for, even when you think you may not have many. You can read, you have an intelligent mind, you are motivated to improve your life—all are positive and real things in your life to be thankful for, among many others.

We also want to encourage you to think of something positive in your life in relation to each of these categories. Perhaps money is really tight right now, but maybe there is something in relation to wealth that you can be thankful for. Perhaps you have good credit—you can be thankful for that. Maybe you have $100 in your wallet—you can be thankful for that. Be thankful for every paycheck or bit of interest earned that comes your way. Maybe you have a house and you really enjoy the great memories that you have created there. You may be asking the universe for a bigger and nicer house, but you can still appreciate what you have right now. Perhaps you want a nicer car—there is nothing wrong with that, but remember to be thankful for the car that you do have.

Do you see what we are doing here? We are looking at each individual situation and finding the good and the positive aspects in each. Being thankful for what you already have creates very powerful vibrations. Powerful and positive vibrations result in the manifestation of what you want to attract! Each positive thought that you create sets off a sequence of vibrations toward the universe. You are telling the universe that you are thankful and that things in your life are good and that you want more of these good things in your life.

Only you can be thankful for what you have—no one else can do it for you. Make sure that the things you are thankful for are those within your control and not someone else's. Be thankful for the job you have. You have that job because of your strengths and achievements. Be thankful for love and support of your family. They love and support you because you are a good and caring person toward them. Be thankful for your good mood. You control your good mood with your positive thoughts and feelings. We are willing to guess that you already have some inspiration in your life. Hopefully by reading this book, we have inspired you to incorporate the LOA into your life. Be thankful that you are inspired to achieve great things.

Realize that all the good things happening in your life are a result of the LOA working for you. Your positive energy has manifested over time and now exists as positive events, things, and thoughts in your life. Now your goal is to make it work for you on a different level, on an infinite level. Being thankful for what you already have will allow you to give off positive energy, which will in turn allow you to attract more and more into your life. The amount of good things you are able to manifest in your life is infinite. Believing that you have already created good and positive energy in your life is important because it helps you realize that you are in control of your present success, and therefore it follows that you are in control of your future success. You are in control of the LOA and what it can do for you. The LOA is working for you now, so you can assume it will work for you in the future and on an even bigger scale. You are a powerful person, capable of attracting anything and everything you want out of life.

YOU CANNOT ACCEPT DEFEAT

It will probably take you some time to get through Step Five—Allowing. For many, there will be time between when you may feel you are completely and utterly allowing anything and everything good into your life, but it has yet to manifest. If you have tried using the LOA in the past, this is the part you have probably given up on. You may feel as though you are doing everything right, but your dreams and goals have not manifested. We are here to tell you: **DO NOT ACCEPT DEFEAT**. Stay the course. Keep thinking positive thoughts. Keep feeling positive emotions. Keep your actions aligned with your purpose. Keep asking the universe for what you want. Ask the universe in various ways, every day, as often as you can.

Realize that your dreams are not necessarily going to manifest overnight. For us, the authors, it took years. But it was a gradual process. Along the way when we would look back, we would think to ourselves, "Wow, I have really accomplished a lot." Our dreams had not fully manifested at many points in time, but they were well on their way. You must be patient with this process.

Admitting defeat closes all doors to the LOA. You have no chance of attracting all your hopes and dreams if you close yourself off from the idea that you can attract things. Do not let yourself give up! The LOA *does* work and it will work for you. You can accomplish great things by incorporating the LOA into your life. Do not accept defeat—we cannot stress how important it is to keep a positive attitude throughout the entire process. Let the following chapter on the Sixth and final step, Receiving, be an inspiration for you.

22

Step Six: Receive It, Enjoy It, Be Thankful for It, Surround Yourself with It

The title of this step says it all. The sixth and final step in the LOA process simply states that once you receive it, enjoy whatever it is that you have asked for and be thankful for it. You should constantly be reminding yourself of how grateful you are. Perhaps it has taken weeks, months, or years to attract the things you want. No matter how long it has taken, realize that you've done it! The LOA works and you now know how to implement it in your life. Enjoy these things that have come into your life. Be careful not to revert to old negative habits. Enjoy what you have and be thankful that you were able to receive it.

Once you have achieved the things you asked for, you will realize how truly powerful the LOA is. It is important for you to continue to believe in the LOA while waiting for the things you desire to come your way. As long as you remain positive and patient, great things will come. The universe is a powerful force—it will reward you with abundance and it will allow you to attract wonderful things into your life.

RECEIVE IT

We believe that this book should be more than just a how-to book. It is fair to assume that you have not received what you have been asking the universe to give to you at this point. But we want you to get used to the idea of receiving the things you wish to attract.

In this step, imagine receiving all the things you have been asking for. You have used all the techniques we have outlined in this book. You have changed your attitude and thought processes from negative to positive. You have figured out what you do not want. You have figured out in great detail exactly what you want and you have incorporated the LOA into your life in every way possible. You have asked in great detail for the universe to give you what you want; you ask every day, as frequently as possible. You have opened yourself up to the LOA and you allow yourself to attract all the things you have been asking for.

The very last step in this process is receiving. Realize that you are not necessarily going to suddenly wake up one day and have everything you have asked for. Some things may come to you instantly, while other things will accumulate over time. It is important for you to see where you are in the process and evaluate your situation accurately. Maybe you have not received what you have been asking for fully yet, but perhaps you will notice that you have come a long way. For example, if you asked for wealth and you have asked to be worth $5 million by the age of forty, perhaps you have accumulated *some* money and you are well on your way to achieving your goal. You are receiving wealth. Another example is your happiness. Perhaps when you first started to evaluate what you wanted to ask the universe for, you asked for pure joy and happiness. After you have successfully completed Steps One through Five, re-evaluate your happiness and examine whether it has improved over time. You will probably notice that it has. Perhaps you have not received pure joy and happiness, but are well on your way toward attracting it.

An example of a clear receipt of something that you might ask for with the LOA might be your dream house or car. There will be an instant in time in which you do not own the house or car and then an instant when you receive it. Imagine receiving something you ask for instantly. Imagine how it would feel to realize that you have attracted what you have been asking for. You should feel strong, happy, proud, and empowered by the LOA. You made the LOA work for you! You can attract anything you want. This can happen with money as well. If you ask for a certain amount of money, it could accumulate over time, or you could receive it instantly.

No matter how you look at it, the LOA is very powerful. You can and will receive anything and everything you ask for. We, the authors, have received what we envisioned many years ago. Now we have new visions and we are asking the universe for these new things. We feel fulfilled, but also realize that with something as powerful as the Law of Attraction, we should aim high and expect to receive the things that we ask for.

ENJOY IT

Enjoying goes along with receiving. You will want to enjoy having and receiving the various things you have asked for. Why do you want to enjoy these things? Well, there was a reason why you wanted change in your life. You have been wanting, asking for, and allowing these things into your life. Now you have what you want, so it is time to enjoy it!

The LOA requires making changes in your life. It requires making an effort to think, feel, and act positively. It requires patience and persistence to keep asking for what you want and allowing everything to come into your life. You have worked hard at attracting all the things you want, and you deserve to enjoy them. Savor all the things that have come into your life. When you receive something into your life that you have been asking for, it is important to take at least a few moments each day and enjoy it. Realistically, the chances are good that you will take more than just a moment out of your day to enjoy what you have received. For example, if you have attracted wealth into your life, every time you make a purchase, pay a bill, or spend money in any way, consciously and deliberately enjoy your ability to spend money. Enjoy having money and wealth as often as possible. It is not necessary to spend money to enjoy it. You can look inside your wallet or look at a bank statement and feel enjoyment in the amount of money you have.

Recall the earlier exercise we mentioned about keeping a $100 in your pocket or wallet and mentally spending the money as often as you like. Perhaps you have done this exercise already. Once you receive wealth into your life, you can enjoy it by doing this same exercise. You can keep a few hundred or a thousand dollars in your wallet and mentally spend it. You can continue to receive, enjoy and increase your wealth by practicing this exercise with even more money.

Another example might be that you have received perfect health from the universe. Now it is time for you to enjoy your perfect health. Acknowledge and enjoy having energy. Enjoy being able to do the things you were unable to when you were not in perfect health. Enjoy having the ability to use your body to go places and do things. Enjoy feeling good and strong. You have been asking for and allowing perfect health into your life for some time. The universe has given you perfect health and now it is time for you to enjoy it!

If you have been granted excellent health, you can also start or continue to exercise. We have already gone over the many benefits of exercise on your health. Incorporating exercise into your life reaffirms to the universe that you are enjoying your perfect health. Always be aware and try to remember that you are very fortunate to have good health and it is important that you use your good health to continue to bring more good into your life. This part of receiving—enjoying what you have received—is easy. Enjoy the changes that have occurred in your life as a result of the LOA. You have worked hard to receive various things, and now it is time to just sit back and enjoy!

BE THANKFUL FOR IT

Being thankful for what you have received should be relatively easy compared to some of the other steps. Instead of putting all your time and effort into asking for the things you wish to attract, after receiving them, you can now be thankful for them. Remember to thank the universe everyday for the things you have been granted with. No matter what position you are in right now, there are things in your life that you should have gratitude for. You should be thankful for some of the things that are in your life right now even if you do not have everything you have been asking the universe for. Know that you are well on your way to receiving everything that you want. In many cases, you must be thankful for what you already have before allowing new things to come into your life. Once you do get the bigger things that you are asking for—the better relationship, the better career, better health—you need to remind yourself on a daily basis of how grateful you are. You need to be aware of, respectful of, and thankful for whatever it is that you have attracted into your life.

Showing the universe your appreciation is an important step in the LOA. Appreciation is extremely powerful throughout this process. Earlier in the book, we encouraged you to be appreciative of things you already have. It is important for you to be thankful for everything you do have, no matter how wealthy, healthy, or happy you are.

When the universe gives you what you have been asking for, express appreciation in as many ways as you possibly can. You can say it out loud or you can say it to yourself, "Thank you." These two words are very powerful. They create positive energy and positive vibrations. You are telling the universe that not only are you appreciative, but that you like and appreciate what you have been given and that you realize how powerful the LOA is. Saying thank you tells the universe that you want to continue receiving wonderful things into your life.

SURROUND YOURSELF WITH IT

This brings us to yet another essential tool and step in the LOA process. Throughout this book you have had the opportunity to learn how to use the six steps of the LOA. We will continue to try to make it as easy as possible for you by sharing what we do on a daily basis to achieve what we want out of life. With this being said, you now know that in order to make the LOA work for you, you have to be very specific about what it is you want, including any and all details, and imagine you already have what you want in your mind on a daily basis. Now you need to surround yourself with it. Negative news and negative people literally poison the mind and stand in the way of your ultimate goals and dreams. Clear your mind of anything negative and create a clear vision of what it is you want and focus on it without interruption. By surrounding yourself with this vision and image on a daily basis, the universe will deliver it to you.

Surrounding yourself with the things that you want to receive and the things you have already received from the universe is a way of telling the universe that you believe in the LOA and you want more. Surrounding yourself also means immersing yourself in everything that you want out of life. If you are asking for a healthy relationship, a stress free life, and good health, then your entire life needs to be surrounded by these things. When you actually receive these things, you will want to keep them and so you must surround yourself with them. The things that you receive from the universe must be an important part of your life. Surrounding yourself with these things tells the universe that you are enjoying these things and that you are thankful to have received them. Realize that surrounding yourself with the wonderful things the LOA has helped to bring into your life creates a domino effect. When you surround yourself with things you have been wanting and things that fulfill you, you create a lot of powerful and positive energy for the universe. The universe will continue to reward you with bigger and better things so that you can create unlimited happiness in your life.

THE POWER OF RECEIVING

Receiving good things into your life is the final step of the LOA. It is not a difficult step, but the process leading up to receiving is the hardest part. Not only must you let positive energy flow into your life, but you must also acknowledge that you have received it. You are the receiver of all the good things that you have asked for and allowed into your life. Once you have received the things you have asked for from the universe, you must be thankful. Receiving, enjoying, being thankful, and surrounding yourself with what you have received is an all-encompassing step. It is a powerful step because it enables you to continue to receive great things into your life.

You must thank the universe for listening to you. You must feel that you fully deserve what has been given to you. Being thankful and appreciative of the things you receive is a very important part of this process. Enjoying what you have is the reason why you are using the LOA, so make sure that you are happy with what you have received and that you enjoy it. The entire concept of the LOA is a process that consists of steps that you must actively work on and incorporate into your life. The end result of this process is that you get what you want. You receive items, become wealthy, abundant, successful, or fall in love. Whatever it is that you want from the universe, you will receive at the end of the process. This book is teaching you attract great things into your life and all of this is accomplished because of you, the universe, and the LOA.

There does not have to be an end to this process. There is no end if you do not want there to be. On one hand you may want very little from the universe and as soon as you receive what you want, you may ask for nothing more. On the other hand, you may use this process for the rest of your life (as we the authors are), so that you are constantly asking for more and receiving more things into your life. We the authors both feel that our potential is unlimited. We have reached the goals that we set out to accomplish with the LOA years ago, but we have both come to the conclusion that there is much more for us to accomplish.

There are so many areas of your life that you can change, expand, and receive new things into. As you go through life, your priorities will most likely change and you can always incorporate the LOA to get what you want. Once you have learned how to use the LOA, you can continue to use it for the rest of your life. Most people agree that life is about changing and improving. The LOA is the perfect process to use in order to continue to change, improve, and grow as a person.

Now, these six steps may sound simple enough. However, the slightest glitch in this process will throw it out of balance. These six steps take practice and it may take quite some time for you to actually implement these steps the way they should be in order to receive and attract from the universe whatever it is that you are asking for. If you find that you are not getting what you are asking for using these six steps, then you need to go back and retrace your steps and re-evaluate because something is off in the process. The LOA, used correctly and with integrity, will give you whatever it is you want and whatever it is that you are asking for...every single time. If you find that it really is not working for you, one of the most common culprits may be that you are focusing too much on what you do not want. For example, a relationship—if you are in a bad relationship and you are constantly focusing on how bad it is, then you are just bringing in more of that bad relationship into your life, which is surrounded in negativity. This is how the process works. If you find yourself complaining on a daily basis about your job—whether you want to change your career or you feel you deserve a raise—then you are attracting more negativity into your life. Let it go. This is part of the process.

The six steps are simple on the surface, but they do require an emotional charge in order to make the LOA work. You may find that some steps seem simpler than others, but there are many details that go far beneath these six steps. It took us, the authors, quite a long time to understand this perfectly and we are still to this day trying to improve this process for ourselves. We know that everything we have been able to accomplish up until this day is because of the LOA.

There are many things that need to be combined with these steps and with the LOA in order to properly make it work for you. You must have the right mindset, as we just mentioned. That is why you have to be very clear. We cannot state this enough throughout this book and entire program. You need to know exactly what it is that you want and you need to focus on it in your mind. You need to have a constant image in your mind of what you hope to achieve or obtain, and a constant focus of what it is that you want. If you want that raise, picture yourself with that bigger paycheck, every single day. Remind yourself every single day of what it would be like to already have that paycheck in your hand. You can even go one step further and imagine where that money from the paycheck would go. Imagine investing some of it or spending some of it on things you want to enjoy. The point is that you follow the six steps, but you tailor them to fit into your life. Make sure you are asking for what *you* want.

23

Self-Hypnosis

Hypnotherapy is a topic that most people are ill informed on. Luckily, Steve Jones, co-author of this book, is an expert in hypnosis and helps many people understand the benefits of learning hypnotherapy and self-hypnosis on a daily basis. In this chapter, we will discuss what hypnosis is, how it will feel to be under hypnosis, what benefits you can gain by learning self-hypnosis, and how it can be used to help in the LOA process.

The first part of this chapter is going to be about hypnotherapy. It is meant to educate on the topic and to help you feel comfortable with hypnosis. The second part of this chapter will be about self-hypnosis. It will help you apply what you have learned about hypnotherapy and teach you how to incorporate self-hypnosis into your life to help you with the LOA.

HYPNOTHERAPY

Let us begin by talking about the four stages of consciousness: beta, alpha, theta, and delta.

Beta: Beta waves are brain waves above twelve Hz (Hz is an abbreviation for hertz, a measure of frequency that is equal to one cycle per second). They are characterized by normal consciousness. As you are reading this book, you are in a beta state because you have thoughts running through your mind and you are able to concentrate on what you are reading. Beta waves represent your conscious and active thoughts.

Alpha: Alpha state is when you are conscious, but your mind is focused on one thing. A good example of this state is when you are driving a car. You are focused on driving, yet still able to react and make decisions on your surroundings. Alpha is the state of self-hypnosis. You can easily train yourself to be in alpha state.

Theta: Theta waves range between four and seven Hz. The theta stage is similar to a deep state of meditation. If you are using hypnosis to make big changes in your life, you will need the help of a hypnotherapist to reach this state as well as a delta state.

Delta: Delta brain waves exist between one and four Hz. They are associated with a deep sleep state.

As you can see from the above information, in order to make changes in your life using hypnosis, it is necessary to be in an alpha or theta state. It is easy for most people to reach an alpha state on their own. It usually takes a trained hypnotherapist to help someone reach a deeper state.

INDUCTION AND DEEPENING

You are most likely wondering how it is possible for you to actually change your brain waves and reach a deeper state. Hypnotherapists use what is known as an induction. It is referred to as an induction because a relaxed state is being induced. An induction is very simple—it is a long, boring, and relaxing story that helps induce hypnosis. The basic requirements of an induction are that it contains elements that include all five of the senses: sight, hearing, smell, taste, and touch. Hypnotherapists use the five senses because different people are relaxed by different senses, and by incorporating all of them, the hypnotherapist is better able to succeed at relaxing a patient.

A deepening is what follows the induction. The deepening gets the client to relax into a deeper state, usually theta. The deepening is usually short and involves a countdown. As the hypnotherapist counts down, they are telling the client to continue to relax. The deepening consists of creating a sense of downward movement. In our first deepening example below, the hypnotherapist asks the client to imagine herself walking down a dune. For each number the hypnotherapist counts down, the client pictures herself walking down and relaxing more deeply. In the second example, the client is asked to imagine the sun lowering on the horizon. The visualization of lowering is a metaphor and is meant to induce a deeper state of relaxation with each step. Both examples come from Steve Jones' book *Inductions and Deepenings: Volume I.*

Example 1: Private Island Induction

Okay now, close your eyes. Let your entire body loosen. Now take three deep breaths. Okay…Breathe in……expand your lungs, filling them with air. That's good. Hold it here for a second…and slowly press it out. Get all of the air out of your lungs. Good, you are feeling more relaxed now. Alright now, breathe in again. Air coming through your nose, feel your chest rise. That's it, really fill up those lungs. Now hold. Open your mouth just a little bit, relax your jaw…and…let out all the air. Slowly release. Feel your chest deflate back down. You are even more relaxed now. Okay, one more time, breathe in slowly. Allow yourself time to fill your lungs. That's good…now hold your breath…and release through your mouth. You are now very relaxed. Not only is your body at ease, but so is your mind. Now, let's take a journey. This journey will involve your five senses and will further relax you. You find yourself on your own private island. You are on the beach. You notice that the island is small, seeing that the beach curves in either direction, surrounding a jungle. Look out at the water. Notice the colors of the water. Picture the clear water. Notice the reef just beyond the sand causes the water to have seven shades of blue and green. You see turquoise, light green, brilliant blue, sea foam green, and several other colors. You look up at the sky and notice how bright blue it is. There are several large clouds in the sky. They are big and white. You notice them move slowly in the sky and change shapes. Watch the clouds as they transform in front of you. The water then distracts you. You notice that about 100 yards in front of you there is a barrier in the water. This barrier is protecting your island and causing the waves to break on it. Listen to the waves hit and break on the rocks. The sound is soothing and you enjoy it. You take a few steps forward and walk into the water. It is completely calm here. The water is warm. Feel it against your legs. The water is soothing to your skin; this relaxes you and puts your mind at ease. You decide to get out of the water. You walk slowly across the beach and into a grove of palm trees. As you walk, a coconut falls from a palm tree just in front of you. You decide to take this coconut and hit it across a rock. This opens the coconut and at first you smell the coconut. It smells sweet and calms you. You then tilt the coconut and taste the coconut milk. It tastes clean and sweet. You leave the coconut behind and continue walking through the palm trees. As you walk, you admire the tall palms swaying in the breeze. You then look in front of you and notice there is a small clearing of trees. In between two trees is a hammock. You decide to lay in this hammock and rest. You climb in and get very comfortable. The hammock sways very gently. As you lay here, you focus on relaxing your entire body. You start with your head. Relax the muscles in your face and in your jaw. Moving down to your neck and shoulders, you relax every muscle. Feel all tension release. Your arms, hands, and fingers lay loosely by your side as you sway on the hammock. Focus on relaxing your core, your lower back, sides, and abs. Now moving further down your body, to your hips and buttocks, you relax these muscles even more. That feels good doesn't it? Relax your thighs. Relax your knees. Relax your calves and shins. Your legs are now completely lifeless. Move down to your ankles, feet, and toes. There is no tension in your feet. Your entire body is now very relaxed. Enjoy this relaxation. Now focus on relaxing your mind. You do not cloud your brain with random thoughts. You focus on relaxing further and enjoying swaying in the hammock. You enjoy this feeling of total relaxation of your body and mind.

Example 1: Private Island Deepening

You easily and effortlessly get out of the hammock and walk a little farther into the jungle of palm trees. All of a sudden, there are no more trees and you are looking out at the ocean while standing on top of a large sand dune. In this sand dune, there is a pathway of ten steps leading down onto the sandy beach. You stand on top of this dune and look down the steps. I will now count down from ten. You will step down each time and as you do so, you will become even more relaxed. You will become more deeply relaxed with every step down that you take. Ten...you are at the top now, feeling relaxed...nine...you take a step down and as you do you are more at ease...eight...deeper now...seven...more deeply relaxed with each step...six...that's good. You are feeling very relaxed. Five...down, down, more relaxed...four...three...you are feeling extremely relaxed now...two...and on the count of the next number you will be completely relaxed...one. You are in a complete state of relaxation. You are now more relaxed than you ever have before. Now we will focus on _____ and you will be ready to make positive changes in your life.

Example 2: Grassy Field Induction

You are lying down and you are feeling very comfortable and at ease. Your eyes are closed. Take a few moments to completely clear your head of any thoughts. Now I want you to take three deep breaths.

Breathe in...inhale...slowly...filling your lungs to capacity...that's good...and now...exhale...releasing the air, letting it out through your mouth. You should feel a little more relaxed. Okay...once again...take a big deep breath. Really fill up your lungs...feel your chest rise...and hold for a second...and exhale...let it all out...slowly. Excellent. Okay, one more deep breath. In through the nose, filling your lungs...now open your mouth and relax your jaw...and release, slowly and barely pushing the air out. Very good. You should be feeling a little more relaxed now. Now imagine yourself in a field. It's a large, grassy field. All the grass around you is a vibrant green color. The grass is very healthy and lush. A warm breeze passes by your body. It feels good and refreshes you. You watch as the breeze causes the grass to sway. It glimmers in the sunshine and looks like waves from the ocean. It sways back and forth, back and forth. The flowing movement of the grass relaxes you as you walk through the grassy field. You hear a hawk making sounds above you. You take a look up at the sky and you spot the brown bird soaring high. You like the sound that it makes; its call is clear and echoes off the mountain. You watch as it circles around above you. You take a look at your surroundings. You are in a valley of grass with a mountain to your left and a mountain to your right. The field where you are is pretty flat. The grass goes a little up the mountains on either side and then the face of the mountains turn to trees. The mountains are capped with snow at the very top. You wonder how tall the mountains are. You are glad that you are warm in the valley below. As you walk around in the grass, you can smell the fragrant sweet smell. You enjoy the smell of grass; there is no other smell quite like it. It smells earthy and natural. You take in a deep breath and relax as you exhale. You continue to walk and continue to relax. You decide to stop for a moment and run your fingers through the grass. The grass feels thick and healthy. It tickles your palm, as you brush your hand on the many blades of grass. You enjoy your time in the field. You take a look at all the colors around you. The grass is a vibrant green and then there is the darker green of the trees up the mountain. Further up the mountain is a grayish-purple hue of rocks and then you see the white of the snow-capped mountains. Beyond the mountains is the bright blue sky. It is a beautiful contrast to the green, grey, and white of the grass field and the snow-capped mountain. There are a few wispy clouds in the sky. They look like quick white brush strokes on a painter's canvas. As you walk through the green grassy field, you come to an area with a large comfortable blanket laying there for you. You lie down on the blanket and close your eyes. You relax your head; every muscle in your face just relaxes. You move your neck around as it loosens. You move your shoulders up and back and let them relax against the blanket. Your arms and hands are resting on the blanket by your side. You begin to relax some more. It feels nice to be in the grassy field relaxing. You then move to your back, going through each vertebra and relaxing the muscles that support your spine. You relax your chest and stomach. You feel your steady breath rising and falling with your chest. You let your hips and buttocks relax into the soft ground below. You move down to your thighs and relax each one. You let your knees part slightly and relax. Your shins and calves relax as you continue to relax your body. You move your feet around and point and flex your toes. This relaxes them and you are in a very peaceful state. Your body is completely at ease. You have nothing on your mind. You enjoy how you are feeling right now. You continue to lay on the blanket in the peaceful grassy field relaxing...

Example 2: Grass Field Deepening

You now slowly sit up and open your eyes and look above at the beautiful mountain and sky. You notice the sun and all the colors on the horizon. The sky is filled with shades of red, orange, pink, and purple. You see that the sun is close to setting behind the mountain to your right. As I count from ten, the sun sets closer to the horizon and you relax deeper and deeper with every number I count. Okay...ten...the sun goes down just a little and you feel yourself relax...nine...you are going deeper into a state of relaxation...you see the sun lower and you are feeling at ease...eight...deeper still...seven...You are feeling more and more relaxed as you watch the sun go down...down...six...you relax further into hypnosis...five...the sun is another step closer to setting behind the mountain and you are very relaxed...four...you relax more deeply...and...more deeply...three...deeper still...you watch the sun go down...down...two...you are very relaxed and at the count of the next number you will be completely relaxed...one...you are very relaxed. You are feeling very comfortable. We will now focus on your subconscious mind to make changes and go forward.

From these examples that we have provided, you should have a general idea of how someone can be induced into a state of hypnosis. Some people are quicker to relax than others.

SCRIPT

The next step in a hypnosis session involves the script. The script is the section of the process that helps reprogram your subconscious mind to make changes in your life. Throughout this book we have included scripts, except that in the case of this book, we have changed the point of view to first person. Scripts consist of a series of suggestions or affirmations aimed at helping people change the way they see things. Instead of having a negative relationship with something, the script acts to create a new positive relationship that replaces the negative. It is a form of reinforcement.

You might be wondering if you would see the same benefit of reading a script versus having the script delivered to you in a state of hypnosis. The answer is no, you would not see the same benefit. When you read a script in a beta state, your conscious mind is receiving the affirmations and suggestions. The bad thing about your conscious mind receiving the script is that it can over-analyze the suggestions and sabotage you. This is what happens when you make excuses or do not meet a certain goal you set out to meet. It can be helpful, as in the case of the LOA, to reinforce positive thoughts, but if the script causes more negative thoughts, then it is not doing you any good. This is why we have introduced the concept of hypnosis in this book. Some people will see better results with the LOA by incorporating hypnotherapy.

Hypnosis targets the subconscious mind when you are in alpha or theta. You are more suggestible in these states. Your subconscious mind does not question the affirmations it hears; it accepts them as true. Your subconscious mind helps you make changes in your life to support the suggestions it is receiving with hypnosis. It will be helpful and important for most people to know that you are always in control while under hypnosis. Many people have the wrong impression of hypnosis, thinking that the hypnotherapist puts you under their control and you relinquish your own. This is incorrect information. You are and will always be in control. You can come out of hypnosis very easily if you choose to.

Hypnosis is not scary. It is very relaxing and calming and often you find that you are alert and aware of what is going on while in a state of hypnosis. During hypnosis, your focus will be more intense and this will allow you to concentrate on making changes in your life. Sometimes people become so relaxed during a session that they fall asleep. This happens often and people usually ask if they will see the benefits of hypnosis if they fall asleep during a session. The answer is yes, you will still see the same benefits. Even while you are sleeping, your subconscious mind stays active and alert, allowing you to absorb the suggestions that the hypnotherapist is giving you.

AMNESIA

Amnesia is the next part of the hypnosis session. "Amnesia" is the part of the session that encourages your conscious mind to forget what it has heard so that it does not over-analyze the words it has heard. All the suggestions the person receives are stored in the sub-conscious mind. The goal of amnesia is to get the conscious mind to forget what was said so that it does not sabotage the benefits. The conscious mind tends to be skeptical and often second-guesses the suggestions. Amnesia prevents this from happening so that the conscious mind forgets what is said and the subconscious mind remembers and starts making changes.

Below is a sample of the amnesia part of hypnotherapy that Steve frequently uses with clients:

> And as you continue to relax, every breath you take is soothing, soothing you. Focus now on your breathing. I wonder how much attention you have paid to the many different thoughts floating through your mind. Your mind is so active even while it relaxes. And then you become aware of how difficult it is to remember what I was talking about exactly seven minutes ago. And you can try to remember what I was saying nine minutes ago or what you were thinking four minutes ago, but doesn't it seem like too much work to try to remember all of that? It takes more effort than it is worth. So relax, relax comfortably and understand that you don't have to remember what I was saying when it is too much work to do. You can choose to remember to forget what I said or to forget to remember what I said. The choice is yours.

As you can see, these words can cause confusion to the analytical mind. This sample is designed to encourage the conscious mind to not try to remember the things that were said because it appears to be too much of an effort. The conscious mind usually decides to not remember, thus making it almost impossible for the conscious mind to second-guess the suggestions in the hypnosis session.

TRANCE TERMINATION

Trance termination is the part of the hypnosis session that ends the trance and it is also when a beta state is restored. A trance termination is meant to slowly bring someone out of hypnosis and back into the "real world." When you awaken in the morning, ideally you would probably like to slowly wake up as your body sees fit. Often it can be jarring to wake up to an alarm clock. Trance termination works to slowly bring you back to a beta state in a relaxing way.

A trance termination is usually fairly short and includes a count of one, two, three. The idea is that at the count of three the person will be out of hypnosis. The hypnotherapist builds their voice to encourage the person out of hypnosis and thus ending the trance. Below is a sample of what a trance termination would sound like. It is an excerpt from Steve's book, *Basic Hypnotherapy for Professionals:*

> Now, in just a few moments, you are going to come back up at the count of three. When I bring you back up, you are going to feel comfortable. You are going to feel relaxed. You are going to feel as though you are out of hypnosis, understanding that your subconscious mind will act on every word you heard during this session. These suggestions will become stronger and stronger in your mind. Over time, these suggestions will become more and more a part of you, and you will become more and more the person of your choosing—a relaxed, calm, confident, peaceful person.
>
> One, beginning to come up, feeling very good, filled with energy, rested, feeling as though you have had a peaceful nap.
>
> Two, coming up even more, beginning to move now, beginning to stir and you are totally at ease.
>
> And at the count of the next number, you will be completely awake.
>
> Three, eyes wide open, relaxed, refreshed, and feeling wonderful.

In an actual session, Steve gives people additional time to sit and relax and ensure they become fully alert after the session and before leaving his office. In his recordings, he does a different kind of trance termination. He ends the trance, but instead of bringing people back up into a state of consciousness or beta state, he suggests they fall into a restful sleep. His recordings are designed to be listened to at night as the client is lying in bed. During the trance termination he says that they will wake up the next morning full of natural energy and ready for a wonderful day.

You should now understand that hypnosis is a safe and natural state. You can make both minor and major changes in your life with the help of hypnotherapy. Many people automatically and incorrectly assume that they are not able to be hypnotized. Hopefully now you have learned that you *can* reach a state of hypnosis and it is no longer a matter in your mind of whether you can or cannot be hypnotized. Everyone can reach a state of hypnosis.

You have also learned that there are varying states of consciousness and that you can be in any of those states while using hypnosis. Alpha state is the easiest to get to and you can see a full range of benefits while in this state. Hypnosis is a powerful tool that can help you make positive changes in your life. Learning self-hypnosis can help you dramatically in incorporating the LOA into your life. Hypnosis directly targets your subconscious mind and can help you to easily master the steps of the LOA that we have outlined in this book.

SELF-HYPNOSIS AND THE LAW OF ATTRACTION

Self-hypnosis is a lot like what we have already described with a hypnosis session led by a hypnotherapist, with the exception that *you* create the session. In this section of the chapter, we will go over guidelines which will help you master self-hypnosis and help you incorporate using the LOA in your life. Remember, whether you are using the guidance of a hypnotherapist or using self-hypnosis, you are always in control.

Your self-hypnosis session can be as short or as long as you would like. We suggest aiming for at least twenty minutes. This time period will allow you to fully relax and focus your subconscious mind on affirmations involving the LOA. Self-hypnosis will take a few practice sessions, but most people find it very easy to learn. In fact, self-hypnosis has been taught to young children and it has been highly successful in cases of asthma (Bray, 2006), ADHD (Barabasz, 2000), and pain relief (Smith, 1996), to name a few. With a little time and practice you will be able to master self-hypnosis. You may find that with repeated use of self-hypnosis, it becomes easier and easier to relax into a state of hypnosis, or you may find it easier to be in a deeper state of relaxation altogether.

Following is the six-step process to your own personal self-hypnosis session. At first you may find that you need to give more time to the relaxation and induction parts to get used to a state of hypnosis. Remember, you are still going to be aware of what is going on around you and you will always be in complete control and able to come out of hypnosis whenever you want.

1. Location

It is important for you to pick a special place that is quiet and where it will be easy for you to become relaxed. This could be anywhere, perhaps in your home or some similar place where you are comfortable. You will want to remain undisturbed, so make sure that there will be no interruptions during self-hypnosis. For example, tell your family not to disturb you and remember to turn off your cell phone. Find a comfortable place where you can sit or lay down and feel at ease. This might be your bed, a comfortable chair, your couch, your floor, or any place you feel at ease.

You might find that with time and practice, you can even perform self-hypnosis in a busy or loud place. You may eventually be able to block out everything around you. You may be able to practice self-hypnosis at work or on an airplane or at any time or location.

2. Relaxation

Relaxation involves preparing your mind and body for hypnosis. You are preparing your mind to go from a busy beta state, where you probably had hundreds of things running through your mind at any given second, to an alpha state, where you are relaxed and focused on one thing...the LOA.

Assuming you are in a comfortable place and can do so, you should close your eyes. You will then want to take some deep breaths and focus on your breathing. Try to divert all attention to your breathing. In this part of relaxation, you are focusing on clearing your mind of all thoughts. As you take a deep breath in, breathe in relaxation and a sense of calm. As you breathe out, imagine getting rid of all negative thoughts, fears, and anxiety. Do this for as little or as long as it takes to dissipate all negative energy from your mind.

You can choose to come up with a relaxation technique of your own, or you can use the following as an example of what you ideally want to be saying to yourself and doing to relax your mind:

> I am sitting in a very quiet place. I go ahead and close my eyes. I pause as I clear my mind of all thoughts. [Pause] Now I take three deep breaths. I breathe in, filling my lungs to capacity, very slowly. And now...I release the air, letting it out through my mouth. I feel more relaxed. Once again, I take a big deep breath, really filling up my lungs. I feel my chest rise. I hold

the breath for a second...and let it all out slowly. Okay, one more deep breath. In through my nose, filling my lungs...now I open my mouth and relax my jaw...and release, slowly and barely pushing the air out. I am feeling a little more relaxed now. I continue to breathe as I normally would. As I breathe in, I focus on relaxing and how good I feel. As I breathe out, I let out all negative thoughts and emotions. I continue to focus on my breathing as I relax...

Next, you will want to focus on relaxing your body. You will want to start with your head and slowly work your way down your body, focusing for a little while on each body part or body zone, relaxing your muscles very deeply. It is important that your muscles are relaxed instead of tense. This will contribute to your overall relaxation and prepare you better for hypnosis.

Below is an example of a full-body relaxation technique. Again, this is just a guide. You can choose to change it however you feel necessary. If focusing more on relaxing the muscles of your face and neck, you can focus longer on this area. The choice is up to you.

I feel my body relax in my comfortable place. I focus on relaxing my entire body starting with my head. I relax my forehead, my face, and my jaw. I feel all the muscles in my face relax. I let my cheeks and the muscles around my eyes and mouth relax. I just sit here for a second and allow my head to be more relaxed than it ever has been before. I relax my neck and shoulders. I let them fall and relax on the surface beneath me. I allow my head to rest easily on top of my neck. I let my arms, hands, and fingers hang loosely by my side. I am feeling very good. I move down my back and down my stomach, letting each muscle loosen. I allow my waist, hips and buttocks to relax. I am relaxing very deeply, all the way to my core. As I continue to relax my upper body, I feel warm and comfortable; it feels nice. I continue on relaxing and focusing on my body. Now I feel my upper legs begin to relax, they become very relaxed. I let my legs fall loosely on the surface beneath me. I move down to my knees, they loosen and become relaxed. I now relax my calves, shins, and all the muscles in my ankles. It feels good to be relaxing. I stretch each toe, one by one. I enjoy feeling this way. I like taking time for myself. I am improving my body and soul by relaxing them. I continue sitting in my comfortable place. I reflect only on how good I feel and how relaxed I am. Other thoughts and memories do not occur to me at this point in time. I continue to lie down and relax.

By now you have properly prepared your mind and body for hypnosis. You have cleared the thoughts from your head and both your mind and body are in a pure state of relaxation. You should be feeling very good and stress free. Realize that the first few times you do these relaxation techniques you may not be able to fully relax your mind and body, but with time and practice you will get better at relaxation.

3. Induction

Remember the induction is a long and boring story that focuses on the five senses. The induction helps induce hypnosis. You can use one of the inductions that we included earlier in this chapter. It also might work better if you think of a story that relaxes you and involves the senses that you are most in tune with. A hypnotherapist uses all five senses because they are not sure which sense appeals most to a person. In your case, you may know that you are primarily a visual or auditory person. Or perhaps your sense of touch or smell relaxes you. Or you can focus on all five—it does not matter. You'll want to think of a five-minute story and imagine it in your mind. This will help you become more relaxed and it will also help you focus your mind on one thing—the story.

Below are some different topics to consider when you think of a relaxing story. Most people find the beach to be relaxing, but you might want a variety of options.

- Beach
- Lake
- Mountain
- Waterfall
- River
- Grassy field
- Outer space
- Scuba diving/snorkeling
- Woods
- City
- Driving
- National Park
- Flying
- Home

You can experiment with these different kinds of stories, or feel free to make one up on a different topic that you find particularly relaxing. It is really based on your personal preference.

4. Deepening

The deepening is an easy concept. Ideally you will want it to correspond with your induction. For example, if you are walking along the beach in your induction, you'll want your deepening to include a lowering that relates in some way to the beach, like the sunset, walking down steps from a pier, or walking down dunes. It is not ideal to have your induction involving one thing and then not have your deepening parallel it in some way. Another example would be if your induction included you being in a city—the deepening could involve you going down floors in an elevator or down stairs in a high-rise building. You can use one of the above examples from above to create your own self-hypnosis deepening. Be sure to include a countdown from ten to one and focus on relaxing as you count down.

5. Script/Affirmations

The scripts or affirmations are the most important part of self-hypnosis. This is where you are going to focus most on making changes in your life. This is where you are going to focus on positive things that you want to incorporate into your life. With the script, it is very important for you not to focus on the negative and not to focus on what you want to stop doing, but rather to focus on the positive and think about the things you want to add to your life.

You can create affirmations to help you incorporate more positive thoughts, feelings, and actions into your life and to change your thought process. You can use self-hypnosis to attract wealth, perfect health, abundance, or material things into your life. The possibilities are truly limitless. You can now incorporate self-hypnosis into everything that you have been focused on attracting with the LOA to create an even more powerful experience.

Using self-hypnosis in conjunction with the LOA allows you to attract many things into your life. You can also focus purely on allowing yourself to attract things. If you are devoting a lot of your time and energy asking for the things you wish to attract, but those things have not come to you yet, then your affirmations might focus on allowance. Allowing positive things into your life is a major part of the LOA. Self-hypnosis can help you open up to allowing all great things into your life.

It might help you to prepare a script or list of affirmations prior to your self-hypnosis session, especially at first. As you practice self-hypnosis, you will get better and better at using the technique to your advantage and affirmations will flow right to you. Self-hypnosis is very therapeutic. It allows you to escape from your day-to-day activities and focus on the LOA. This form of therapy also creates a lot of positive energy. While you are practicing self-hypnosis, the universe will take notice of your vibrations.

6. Trance Termination

You can come up with a simple trance termination to help you return to your normal beta state. All you have to do is count to three and come out of hypnosis. You will want to use the same techniques a hypnotherapist would use, as we explained before. You will want to slowly count to yourself starting with one and becoming more aware of your surroundings as you count up to two and three to yourself. Here is a basic trance termination you can use after you are finished with your script and positive affirmations:

> One, beginning to come up, feeling very good, filled with energy, rested, feeling as though I have had a peaceful nap. (Pause).
>
> Two, coming up even more, beginning to move now, beginning to stir, and feeling totally at ease. (Pause).
>
> And at the count of the next number, I will be completely awake and alert.
>
> Three, eyes wide open, relaxed, refreshed, and feeling wonderful.

Something to keep in mind with self-hypnosis is that it is possible that you can fall asleep. If you think falling asleep is a possibility, we suggest you set an alarm clock to wake yourself up if you want or need to wake up by a certain time. As your self-hypnosis skills improve, you will be able to shorten your relaxation, induction, and deepening stages thus lowering your chance of falling asleep.

We hope that you have found this chapter on hypnotherapy very informative and hopefully we have debunked some common misconceptions. Hypnosis is really this simple—it is nothing scary. Again, despite what many people think, everyone can achieve a state of hypnosis. You will always be in control while in a trance. Hypnotherapy is safe, natural, relaxing, and a great tool to use to help incorporate change in your life. We hope that you will make self-hypnosis a part of your everyday life, as hypnosis is a terrific and highly effective tool to help you get the most out of the LOA. Self-hypnosis will allow you to focus your attention on the LOA without any other distracting thoughts or feelings. When you focus all of your attention and energy on one thing, you are creating very positive vibrations for the universe. Your focus on the LOA becomes many times more powerful with hypnosis.

Your positive thoughts are hundreds of times more powerful than your negative thoughts. When you focus your energy for twenty or thirty minutes a day using self-hypnosis, you are creating positive thoughts that are working to your advantage. Being successful with the LOA is very important to all that use it. We have found hypnosis to be a great tool to use to promote attraction in our lives. We hope that you see the importance of controlling your subconscious thought and we hope you see just how powerful hypnosis can be with the LOA.

24

Incorporating the Exercise of Silence

*"Power comes through repose; it is in the Silence that we can
be still, and when we are still, we can think, and thought is
the secret of all attainment."*

—Charles F. Hannel, *The Master Key System*

The exercise of experiencing silence is another key tool that goes
hand in hand with obtaining successful results through the LOA. You
will find that taking time out to experience a moment of calming
silence enhances the powers of the LOA. Silence and meditation insu-
lates you from negativity and allows you to receive results faster. In
the rush of modern life, many of us never take any time out to truly
appreciate stillness. Almost every moment is fraught with running
around, trying to accomplish things, getting stuck in traffic, and being
distracted with one thing or another. Ever since the dawn of laptop
computers and cell phones, we are also constantly connected to the
digital world. There is little time when we are not hearing the cell
phone ring or checking our email.

One element important to the LOA that we often miss in daily life
is incorporating a ritual of silence or meditation. All of the day-to-day
commotion we experience is in fact a form of noise pollution that distracts us from our core energy. When we are distracted, it sometimes
becomes harder to listen to our intuition or pick up on the signals that
the universe may be giving us to guide us toward our desires.

Both the root and the key to our success in life always come from within. Silence and the LOA work hand in hand. When we are running around, distracted by everyday life, we fail to connect with our subconscious mind. By setting time aside to experience silence, we also give ourselves the vital opportunity to connect with our subconscious. Our subconscious is always accessible to us, and it always holds great knowledge that our conscious minds do not have access to on a daily basis. When you think about it in this fashion, it is actually a bit amazing that everyone does not take time each day to sit in silence and convene with their subconscious.

GETTING STARTED WITH A PRACTICE

Everyone living in the modern world is inevitably going to get caught up with distractions. There may always be things going on in your life and you may not always enjoy doing all of them. However, if you can incorporate a daily practice of stillness into your life, whereby you just sit and appreciate pure bliss, more of this bliss is what you will receive. Indeed, the more we meditate, the better we will become at turning off our thoughts. At first it may seem difficult to apply this practice to your daily life. Many people give up in the beginning because they find that instead of sitting calmly or euphorically, they are sitting with worried thoughts racing through their minds. Ironically, they potentially begin worrying more about the fact that they cannot get rid of the worried thoughts!

If you want to enhance a feeling of well being during your exercise of silence, try visualizing something simple that is peaceful for you—waterfalls, a sunny day, snow falling…whatever works for you. You might want to choose some soothing music to play in the background that calms you and heightens a trancelike state for you. If you find that you are thinking or worrying when practicing silence, it is important to focus on breathing deeply. With each breath, try to become more and more calm. Once you have slowed your breathing, you will find that your thoughts also slow down.

If you do start thinking any new thoughts, try not to stress about the situation. Instead, simply acknowledge that you are thinking distracted thoughts (whether they are good or bad), and allow yourself to go back to silencing your mind. It is important to realize that it is normal for thoughts to surface when we are being still and silent. Our brains are designed to have thoughts continually run through them, and this is normal. However, you will find that with practice, each time you meditate you will be able to truly turn off your thoughts with increased ability.

HOW SILENCE COMPLEMENTS THE LAW OF ATTRACTION

Where the LOA is involved, it is vital to connect with your deepest thoughts for a variety of reasons. First of all, if our thoughts and feelings are creating our reality, we need to spend more time feeling happiness and bliss. When we are in stillness we can truly experience moments of bliss, free of thought. In fact, monks have professed to have even have reach states of nirvana during meditation! The more time we spend feeling blissful, according to the LOA, the more bliss we will attract into our lives. When thinking of it this way, it seems only logical that you would want to incorporate meditation into your life. Any safe and healthy tool or method that gives you more inner joy is something that you need to explore.

There is little doubt from scientific studies that have been done on meditation and stillness that experiencing the feelings that come with doing so relieves feelings of stress and enhances well being. Even if you aren't experiencing nirvana during meditation, you still will receive the health and wellness benefits that meditation offers.

Another masterful thing that stillness offers that complements the LOA is respite from our thoughts. As we discussed in previous chapters, negative thoughts lead to things showing up in our lives that we do not want. However, meditation, silence and stillness have the remarkable ability to let us escape from our thoughts. Often when people are first introduced to the LOA and start practicing it, they fall into a trap of letting their brain obsess about things and actually wind up working too hard. For example, it is common for people to have a bad day, think negative thoughts and then fall into a downward spiral. Another common problem is thinking about something negative and then panicking that those negative thoughts and feelings will draw bad things your life. Once you start panicking, the negative thoughts that ensue can truly lead to things you do not want happening.

Another tendency that many newcomers to the LOA often fall into is not allowing the results to be easy. Many people are accustomed to working hard and even to struggling, so much so that even good things in their lives (like the LOA) tend to feel stressful instead of good. It is common to worry about not following the LOA steps well enough. All of the steps can seem overwhelming at first, and some people worry if they miss one step or forget to do part of the process accurately, their work will fall apart.

The practice of silence also helps tremendously when you begin to worry or obsess about results or fall into perfectionist thinking. Yes, the LOA may have a lot of steps to follow at first. However, if we are always stressing about results, it becomes too difficult to simultaneously be and feel positive. Meditation and silence allow us to release that stress.

Another benefit to the addition of silence into your daily routine is that it calms your nerves and improves your reactions to everyday occurrences. All in all, you will find your sense of focus and relaxation increasing as you cultivate this practice. You will see these results not just when you are meditating, but also throughout the day. Once you start a daily silence exercise you will probably find that little things do not bother you as much as they may have previously.

DETACHMENT

Meditation and observing silence gives you a sense of what can best be called detachment. You will find that you do not feel as deeply attached to and impacted by situations that would have intensely drawn you into them in the past. It is an amazing feeling to loosen your hold on ideas and situations that previously would have impacted you negatively.

Detachment ties in profoundly to the LOA. When we get caught up in life's stressful moments, the potential is always there to start a downhill spiral, so to speak. For example, imagine you get to work one morning and read a negative memo directed at you. If your emotions and thoughts turn negative due to this occurrence, the LOA can bring you a related series of negative events and corresponding negative thoughts. After reading this memo, your pulse races, stress chemicals run through your system and you find yourself in a bad mood. Throughout the day, you might have a fight with a co-worker, you might accidentally drop your cup of coffee and stain your clothes or burn yourself, and you might make mistakes during your workday that lead to other unfortunate events for you. Even without any sort of mysticism involved, it is easy to see on a very practical and pragmatic level that one bad thing does tend to lead to another.

Imagine again that same person who received the negative memo in the morning. In this case, however, the individual has been practicing silence and stillness everyday. When this person gets the memo, instead of allowing it to negatively impact him, he will face the situation with a certain sense of detachment. There is a sense that this is just an experience being faced. As a result, the experience does not throw this person off balance. The situation may even be looked at with a certain sense of amusement or lightheartedness. Perhaps there is something this person can learn on some level from the memo. This person will assimilate all of these things, and the experience would not potentially get him "bent out of shape." As a result, the LOA might bring this person more interesting and humorous incidences throughout the day. One of the primary things to learn with the LOA is how to control your thoughts and feelings. A routine exercise in which you practice stillness allows you to cultivate this ability to better control your reactions. When you react to things quickly with anger or rage, you are no longer the creator of your thoughts.

Remember, you are the creator of your life. As a result, it goes unsaid that you would of course want to have total control over the emotions and feelings that you experience as the result of something happening to you. At this point in your life, you simply want to create success and manifest your goals. You do not want to get caught up in pettiness or silly games. It is surprising how many adults spend inordinate amounts of time trying to be hurtful or manipulative of others' emotions. It is evident, and unfortunate, that many of us operate on the same emotional level as preadolescents, and sometimes even worse.

It is difficult to overstate just how important it is that you learn how to distinguish between what is important to focus on and what is not important to focus on for the LOA to work successfully. Learning to avoid the silly games that many people in our society play is not an easy lesson to learn. From a young age we are taught that it is important to be popular, to be well liked, to do what we are told and so on. Often, however, doing these things can be in direct conflict with what is best for you. Sadly most adults still operate on a petty level, often responding disproportionately to stressful situations that arise.

Learning to prioritize is another one of the most important things you can do to make the LOA work for you. Think about it. If you are prioritizing trivial and petty concerns, you are not focusing on the goals that you have in life. For example, if your goal in life is to become wealthy or lose weight, you have to stop and ask yourself if your thoughts, words and actions are reinforcing those goals. By seeking out revenge or gossiping, just to cite two examples, how have you progressed your goals?

The LOA is all about having your goals progress. You have to want success; you have to want to have your goals met. A key part of finding this success is to understand that you must stay focused on what is positive, affirming and progressive. Negative emotions, such as revenge, are emotions that will not attract anything positive into your life. If you are thinking about negative things, you are simply not focusing on your job at hand—the job of becoming the best person you can be and achieving your goals. Most people do not think of themselves as being a possible factor that may get in the way of their own success. Most of us think of the obstacles that we face as being strictly external, but often the obstacles that are the most difficult ones to overcome are the ones that we cannot even see. If you are your own worse problem, then you are likely to need a fresh perspective in order to understand what it is exactly that you are doing that is detrimental to your own success.

Meditation and silence are essential in combating the obstacles to success that you may have, usually unwittingly, created for yourself. When practicing silence, you can begin to reflect upon your actions and see your actions in a way that you would normally not see them. In a very real sense, you are "getting out of yourself." Meditation can alter your consciousness and help you get in touch with parts of your mind that you are normally unaware of on a day-to-day basis. Phrased another way, meditation can help you achieve your goals by clearing your mind enough to examine where you may be obstructing your own growth. Most of us have heard that "perception is everything." This is part of why meditation and silence are so important to the LOA.

Experiencing silence in your life also leads to a sharper ability to listen and respond to your intuition. Opportunities and signals that will guide you toward success constantly manifest. If we are caught up in distractions, emotions or negative feelings, we often won't even notice these opportunities and wonderful moments. If we are too distracted to see them, they will often pass us by. Practicing silence will greatly assist you in your quest to focus on all that is good and positive. It will also help you focus on those things that you can change or steps you can take to make certain that you will reach your goals.

HEALTH BENEFITS OF MEDITATION

If you still need more convincing, consider that modern medical science is learning more about the physical benefits of meditation every day (Carmody & Baer, 2008). Medical science now sees the benefit to such practices as meditation and acupuncture. There was a time that Western medicine did not see the benefit of these practices, but in recent decades the value of meditation has become more and more obvious. Meditation is, in fact, a very important tool for anyone who is using the LOA. It is very clear that meditation can benefit you and your goals in a wide variety of ways.

Though you may not realize it, meditation and the practice of silence can actually protect both your body and your mind. Scientists have discovered that meditation is a very effective way of reducing the stress hormones in our body that cause aging. Stress causes your adrenal glands to produce cortisol, and cortisol literally ages your body. Excess cortisol, such as that released by stress, has been proven to weaken the human immune system. Numerous medical studies indicate that stress has a massive impact on both body and mind. This is yet another way that meditation can help you meet your goals and achieve your dreams.

One of the key ways to combat this stress hormone and its harsh effects on your body is through meditation and diet. Meditation is highly effective in fighting the negative effects of cortisol, for when you meditate, your heart rate slows down and your body naturally becomes calmer and more relaxed. This translates into—meditation can actually mean less diseases and sickness in your life. This fact should strike you as nothing sort of incredible. Why wouldn't you meditate? The immunity strengthening benefits alone are enough to justify taking fifteen minutes out of a day to do so. When you are ill or sick, you are not usually at your highest level of productivity. Think about your major accomplishments in life. How many of these accomplishments came while you had a severe cold or flu, for example? The odds are good that not too many of your accomplishments happened when you were very ill.

This link between meditation and physical illness is a very significant one and plays directly into the LOA. If you are sick, you are not likely to feel much like working, let alone being innovative or creative. Meditation relaxes the mind and the body. Muscles relax and the mind is allowed a few moments to "turn off." It may sound bold, but the truth of the matter is that by not meditating you are making your job of achieving what you want more difficult. Remember that the LOA means that you will attract more of what you are focusing on into your life. If you want positive things to flow into your life, you are making that process more difficult by not being as happy and relaxed as you can be. Meditation will alter both your body and your mind in a positive way. It will readjust your mind in ways that will increase your ability to attract what you want into your life.

Meditation is a powerful tool that can be used to help you achieve your goals. People who mediate often feel as though they are not just healthier, but calmer, more confident and creative. Calmness, confidence and more creativity are all attributes that virtually anyone who is trying to achieve more in life would want. Who wouldn't want to be more creative, for example? How foolish and arrogant would it sound to hear someone say, "I am creative enough, I would hate to be more creative"? Most people would think that anyone saying this was either a little insane or incredibly arrogant.

Imagine stopping people on the street and telling them that you have a free way to make them for relaxed, healthier and more creative. Most will have trouble believing you and think that you are trying to sell them something. Now imagine how shocked the average person would be when you told them that the "secret" is meditation. By realizing all the myriad ways that meditation and the power of silence can help you meet your goals, don't you feel that you have been given a significant piece of information?

The ability to make good, quick decisions is often a characteristic that is attributed to great leaders throughout history. Being able to discern between what is important and what is clutter is vital to anyone's success. Good leaders can quickly distinguish between the important and the trivial. Meditation can help in bringing about a great focus of the mind, making one's mind calmer and clearer. It might seem a little funny to think of your mind as an ocean, but the analogy does work. Try to think of your mind as an ocean and your goals as a boat in that ocean. A chaotic mind means rough seas and a calm mind means smooth sailing, so to speak. Which ocean is easier to travel on?

With your mind calmed, you may find that many of the problems that currently confound or frustrate you now may simply just melt away. Further, you may find that you are able to think more clearly and make decisions in a quicker fashion. Being able to make good and quick decisions is something that goes hand in hand with achieving your dreams via the LOA.

While you may be convinced that meditation can help you, you may still be worried about finding the time to meditate on a regular basis. After all, there is no doubt that modern life can be very hectic. No matter who you are or what you do, it can be difficult to find those fifteen minutes of quiet to spend just meditating. Let's consider an extreme example. You are a working mother with three children, ages three, seven and ten. That is a handful. How can you find time? The first step is to obviously make it a priority. Tell your husband that you are taking a bath for fifteen minutes and that you are going to listen to music through headphones to relax. You can even use earplugs. You do not even have to tell anyone that you are meditating. Even if someone walks in on you, they may simply think you are simply relaxing, which, of course, you are.

The odds are that most of us have a few time wasters that we can eliminate and replace with meditation. Spend five or ten fewer minutes on the phone with family or friends. Skip a second-rate television show that you often say you should not watch anyway, or find some other way to squeeze fifteen or twenty minutes out of the day. There is likely a way—if you want it enough. In order to achieve your goals, the odds are great that you will need strong discipline and a keen ability to concentrate. No doubt, somewhere lost in history is a man or a woman with greater mental gifts than Einstein or Newton, who lacked their powers of concentration and discipline. Meditation and the exercise of silence will help sharpen your mind in order that you can pursue your dreams with more vigor.

25

Extra Tools for Setting the Law of Attraction into Motion

"Once you make a decision, the universe conspires to make it happen."

—Ralph Waldo Emerson, 1803–1882

There are a variety of effective tools that will help you to get the best and fastest results with the LOA. You will find that there is a wide array of tricks and techniques people have used to draw wealth and abundance to themselves. Sometimes when you are starting out with a new way of thinking and perceiving the world around you, it is a good idea to incorporate tools and games into your life to keep it all fun, and stimulate your mind and imagination.

Remember, since the LOA draws upon your own good feelings and vibrations, it is beneficial to make sure that any tools you use are enjoyable for you during the process. Periodically, make it a priority to take a moment to reflect and make sure you are having fun. If you begin to feel like any of these tools are difficult, or if you start taking anything too seriously or perceive it as "hard work," you may very well be on the wrong path. We have already discussed a few popular tools such as creating vision boards, making wealth boxes, and keeping $100 bill in your pocket and practicing thinking of how to spend these bills (just to name a few tips we have gone over in this book so far). As countless people have had amazing results with the LOA, to this date there have been countless new techniques and ideas developed. This chapter will explore some of the other tools people have used to get the LOA to work.

As with many things in life, you will find that some of these tools are a great fit for you and some are less interesting and successful. Even if techniques and tools do not specifically work for you, do not give up. There are undoubtedly some tools that will fit your personality type perfectly. While exploring these tools, again just be sure to try to enjoy yourself as much as possible. If you find something is not working, just move onto the next tool.

VISUALIZATION MOVIES

Many people have begun developing visualization movies as an alternative to vision books. Visualization movies, sometimes also referred to as "Mind Movies," take vision books to the next level and create a multimedia experience based on your own thoughts and goals. You can consider visualization movies to be the "vision book 2.0." The basic concept behind visualization movies is that when your inspiring desires and goals become a multimedia experience, it is easier to get caught up in the dream and believe it is real. When we watch movies, we often get completely caught up and believe the story wholeheartedly. Why else would we cry at the sad parts of a movie and laugh at the funny parts?

Similarly, the visualization movies seek to enhance our belief in our visions far beyond what we would read in a book. Visualization movies incorporate the images of your dreams, along with inspiring music and your own inspiring words or quotes. This is your chance to really be creative and produce your own film that forecasts you achieving your goals and dreams. When you sit down and watch your own visualization movie, your thoughts and goals come to life and are lifted off the page and into reality.

Software is available for purchase online that allows you to create your visualization movie in a streamlined fashion. Yes, you can purchase an actual piece of software that is specifically dedicated to putting together a visualization movie if you wish. It is also very easy to put together this type of film with any generic editing software that comes with your computer. As you are putting together your movie, we suggest including photos of places, items, relationships and goals that you seek. Choose a soundtrack of music that inspires you and makes your heart soar, and feel free to include inspiring quotations that stimulate your inspiration or confidence in the LOA. Then, take these elements and edit them together in a manner that pleases you. Make sure that you let your subconscious guide you toward putting together something that works for you. The editing and technique does not have to be perfect—this video can be as amateurishly done as you want. The important thing is that the video inspires you and lifts your spirits whenever you view it.

Similar to a vision book, it is important to view your visualization movie as much as you can in order to integrate it into your life and allow you to start believing. Watch it in the morning, afternoon and before you go to bed if possible. Seeing your own goals play out in this movie will cement your feelings that these achievements are yours already. Watching the film will get you used to believing that these goals have already been accomplished—a major part of the LOA.

Remember that one of the keys to the LOA is to feel as though what you are seeking is already yours. Often people fail at using the LOA because they end up feeling a longing type of emotion about the fact that they do not already have what they are seeking. Sometimes it is hard for people to get past that feeling, when what they want is not yet theirs. However, if you are feeling emotions of *wanting* and feeling unfulfilled, that is what you will be sending out to the universe. As a result, you will receive more lack and want back into your life.

The visualization movie is a great tool for allowing you to feel all the powerful feelings that you have achieved what you want (without experiencing a sense of yearning or want). When you are watching the film, you can lose yourself in it and the emotions it evokes completely. This process allows you to get out of your head, where you could potentially have the emotions of fear, frustration or lacking.

SCRIPTING

Another powerful tool for bringing the LOA into your life successfully is called scripting. In this process, you write about the future as if it were taking place in the present. You might want to get out a pen that you particularly like, and then the process is simply to write what you want to achieve. The process of writing all of this down, or *scripting*, helps to put energy and intention into your desires and also clarifies your goals. Your emotions and thoughts will be sparked during the writing process.

As you are writing, picture your desires. Similarly to many other exercises involving the LOA, visualization is very important to the success of the process. Once you have written down the basics, go ahead and add in lots of details. While writing, of course, feel as though this desire has already come into being. Write everything in a manner that allows you to feel good. You will feel the positive energies flowing through you. Feel free to include in your script why you want this goal. The more positive thoughts and emotions you include in your script, the better the process. This exercise is very simple, but also very powerful. Remember, some of the simplest exercises are also the most effective. Not everything has to be complicated!

Also remember to keep in mind that your job is not to find out why something will not work, your job is to find a way to make it work. That is always your job, to find a way to make your life the one that you want. This exercise will also help you identify what the correct steps may be that you may need to take in order to make your dreams into a reality.

MASTER MIND GROUP

Another tool that countless individuals have used in order to get the LOA jumpstarted toward helping them achieve their goals is a Master Mind Group. As we have discussed, surrounding oneself with a group of likeminded individuals is of utmost importance. It is crucial to be with people who are exploring and seeking similar goals. A Master Mind group consists of a group of like-minded people who meet to support one another in goals of success.

Remember, few things can bring you down quicker than being with people who express negative beliefs and thoughts. However, many people are so accustomed to being with the people they usually spend time with that they are not sure how to go about finding new friends with similar expectations and outlooks. One of the ways you can quickly find likeminded individuals, and even likeminded people who care about you and want to help you, is by joining a Master Mind group.

With the Master Mind Group, the idea is not only to get advice and support from people who not only have similar intents, but also to surround oneself with likeminded and positive individuals. The group members will all be able to share their success stories during each meeting, and empower one another through the process of sharing positive results. The group can become a great place to celebrate one another's successes and keep up accountability toward commitments. In many cities, it is easy to find a Master Mind group to join online.

You may find results simply by cross-referencing the terms "Master Mind Group" and the name of your city into your web search engine. You might be pleasantly surprised to find out that Master Mind groups are currently forming and looking for new members. If you find that you are having trouble locating a group to join, why not start your own? The best size of a group would be five or six people. The group can either meet in person or communicate over the phone in a conference call. During the meeting, every person will share stories of success and what they are working on. The other members of the group are encouraged to give feedback and guidance or answer questions.

Creating a new group where everyone is new and starting at the same level can be an even more empowering experience. By these means, you get to choose the members that you think will be the best fit, and perhaps even appoint yourself the group leader. This process would be a great way to work on your leadership abilities and your ability to manifest great results.

Napoleon Hill first coined the term *mastermind alliance* in his classic book *Think and Grow Rich* (1987). Hill described it as "two or more minds working actively together in perfect harmony toward a common definite object." Since that day, people have been effectively forming Master Mind Groups to achieve goals.

EMOTIONAL FREEDOM TECHNIQUE

Emotional Freedom Technique, or EFT, is another tool that can work hand in hand with the LOA. EFT is a method based on the theories of acupuncture that activates the body's energy meridians to free painful emotions from the past. The science behind the Emotional Freedom Technique is that the body's energy field consists of electrical impulses. This energy field can get accidentally blocked or misaligned, resulting in a block of a positive flow of energy. When we are out of balance there is often blocked energy that is disrupting the regular pathways of the body. EFT consists of a sequence of tapping on a series of points on the body, which thereby releases these blocks, which are often caused by disrupted energy from traumatic events from the past.

So how does EFT work hand in hand with the LOA? Sometimes people find it is not easy to switch into focusing on the positive to make good things happen. They are stuck in negative emotions or thoughts about what happened to them in the past. Often, past programming puts people in a mindset where they believe that it is not possible to achieve something that they want. When people's emotions are blocked, the Emotional Freedom Technique can be a great method for releasing their stuck energy. By tapping on meridian points, the fear or confusion surrounding a situation can be released. Once energy is flowing freely, people are better able to achieve what they want via the LOA.

When energies and emotions are stuck, even all of the positive thinking and positive emotions in the world sometimes won't necessarily bring someone what he or she wants. Blocked energy can be very detrimental as the person's subconscious is not in agreement with what the conscious mind wants. In order for the LOA to work, the conscious and subconscious minds must be working in harmony. People can write all the positive scripts and make all the vision boards they want, but if their emotions are not in alignment with their thoughts, it will be difficult for the good results to come through quickly or at all. What we want to achieve when we use the LOA in our lives is to have no barriers in our thinking, feelings or actions. It is when we think, feel and act in an unencumbered manner that amazing results come through the fastest.

The Emotional Freedom Technique has the potential to reframe your thinking into positivity. The LOA gives you more good things in your life when you focus on the positive. If the EFT can keep you from recalling or being submerged in the negative, the LOA can then proceed to bring you want you want in an unhindered fashion. When you use EFT to release your inner conflicts and residual negativity, the LOA is freed up to bring you what you want.

TITHING

Tithing is another technique that enhances the universe's ability to give you what you want through the LOA. The main idea of tithing is to give away part of your income in a voluntary manner. Often this tends to be ten percent of your income. Many people give money to causes that they deeply care about and in turn, use the laws of karma to receive good into their own lives. The act of tithing must be done through a genuine feeling of abundance and desire to give to others.

When you give money to others, you are making a clear statement that you believe in the constant flow of money to yourself as well. You feel that you can give freely because your own supply of money will be consistently replenished. In fact, this rule is the truth. When you give your money freely, new money will come back round into your life. Tithing stimulates our feelings of abundance, thereby allowing us to overcome feeling and thinking scarcity thoughts. By tithing, you are helping to reprogram your mind to stop feeling that you do not have enough money by giving it away freely.

Traditionally, the term *tithing* applied to giving at a church. However, the tithing of today can apply to giving money to any charity, person or cause that you believe in. Use your imagination as to whom you want to tithe to. Perhaps you want to give money to someone who would never be expecting a donation. One technique you can use to tithe would be to leave dollar bills in places where someone will come along and find the money later. You can even leave positive messages with the bills to bring other people hope and joy. You can write notes and attach them to the bills, with statements such as "Believe that good things will happen to you!" or "Use this money to do something good for someone else." When you leave money for other people without expecting anything in return, it will stimulate the flow of good into your own life.

COMPLAINT-FREE HOLIDAY

Another technique you can use to practice bringing the LOA into your life is what we like to call a complaint-free holiday. So what is this holiday and why have you never heard of it before? Well, the complaint-free holiday is a day in which you carefully monitor what you say. All day long, you make it a vow to utter no negative statements out loud. By monitoring yourself carefully to not say anything negative all day, you will notice that your thoughts also become more positive as a result. When you realize that you cannot complain or say anything negative, you will find that your thoughts consequently step up to the plate to support you in your goals. It may be useful to think of this complaint-free holiday as a game at first. Can you see how many hours you can go without thinking or saying something negative? The results likely will surprise you.

At first, trying this exercise might seem unrealistic. After all, are there not negative statements that need to be uttered on a daily basis? The answer to that question, of course, is no. We *think* that we need to speak in negativity, because we see so many other people doing this around us. However, in order to get the LOA to work for you, it is much more beneficial to think and act in the way which is most beneficial to your own life and ignore what other people happen to be doing.

Another interesting aspect of the complaint-free holiday is that once people begin paying attention, most are extremely surprised at just how many negative statements they make on a routine basis. Quite a few people have entered into this experiment with the preconception that they do not complain much at all. Often, people have very unrealistic ideas about how they themselves think and act. However, once they begin to monitor what they actually say, they find that they are far more negative than they even realize.

Habitually thinking negative thoughts and making statements throughout the day that are less than positive are automatic processes that are entrenched in many people's lifestyles, so much so that they do not even realize it is happening. It is only by taking time out to consciously monitor our patterns do we become aware of their existence.

This complaint-free holiday exercise can often be extremely eye opening. If you attempt this experiment, you will find out exactly how much negative thinking you have going on that you are not even aware of. How else can you change a habit that you don't even realize exists? Of course, you cannot change your thinking until you notice what it is to begin with. If you try the complaint-free holiday exercise for just one day, you may be shocked at the results. These negative thoughts and complaints are bad for other people *and* for you. Recall Dr. Emoto's experiment mentioned earlier in the book, where he labeled bottles of water with positive and negative statements, and how it changed the water's very make-up. If you are labeling yourself or others with negative words or thoughts, it is just as negative for them—and you.

It is not a good idea to tell yourself and others, "I am tired," "I don't feel good," "I don't like my life," and so on, when you know that these statements will only be reinforced in your mind and to the universe when you make them. Additionally, the LOA will only be drawing more of a similar vibration to you when you make these statements.

During your complaint-free holiday, see if you can achieve the goal of not uttering one negative statement all day. At first, this exercise may seem impossible. Eventually, you will see that it becomes easier and easier to retrain your thoughts and your words to lean toward the positive.

Once you have mastered one day of a complaint-free holiday, try to let go of making any negative statements for an entire weekend. At first this may seem impossible as well. Once you have managed to release all complaints for three days, try a week, a month, or even a year. Ideally, the goal is to eventually let go of complaining and making negative statements for an entire lifetime. The complain-free holiday can also help you in a variety of other ways. Negative thoughts are simply not good for our health, and have even been proven to have an impact on the strength of our immune systems—this can leave us open to all sorts of illnesses. You may find that once you start your complaint-free holiday, you will have more energy and feel happier in general.

If you can let go of making negative statements, you can and will see positive results in your life in many ways. You are letting go of the negative patterns that have had a hold on you, and as a result you are opening the door to attracting all of your goals and dreams into your life. These are goals and dreams that were actually being hindered by the negativity that existed in your thoughts and your speech patterns—before you knew how to effectively use the LOA to change them.

WHAT CAN I DO WITHOUT?

Another interesting exercise is to simply think through your lifestyle and determine what it is that you need and what you do not need. Many people never achieve their goals in life because they are slaves to social norms and their material possessions. You may find that it would be infinitely easier to achieve your goals and use the LOA if you were not so weighed down by your lifestyle. Eliminating unnecessary expenses and physical possessions might make your job easier.

Often the key "move" in life is to know what questions to ask yourself and when to ask. One important question you may need to ask yourself is whether or not you need the things that you have. To be honest, for most of us, most of our major "possessions" are not really our own. This may be depressing but it is true. Most of us do not really own our house and by the time most of us pay off our car, it is often time for a new one.

You may feel that you are just fine with the way things are and that is okay. But you do need to ask yourself, "Do I own the objects I think I own? Do these objects and material possessions make me happy? Do they interfere with my ability to strive for my goals and use the

Law of Attraction?" Take an afternoon to go through your closet and fill a bag with everything that you no longer need. In fact, fill as many bags as you can with items that no longer benefit you. Donate these items to charity so that they can benefit someone else's life. Giving away possessions is a great way of breaking with the old in your life, and bringing in the new. If you have clothes or possessions that you no longer wear or use frequently, what is the point of holding on to them? Many of these items may hold negative energy that ties you to past events and thoughts that no longer serve you. The LOA will be bringing all kinds of new and exciting possessions into your life, so clear out the space to get ready to bring in the new.

26
Conclusion

We hope that you have learned a lot about the LOA in this book. We the authors feel that the LOA has gotten us to where we are today. As a result, we feel the need to spread as much information about it as we possibly can. We both consider ourselves and each other to be a success. We both look back at what we have been able to accomplish in five years and find it astounding. We attribute our success to using the LOA. We found that by incorporating the LOA in one area of our lives, we were successful, and it followed to incorporate it in all areas of our lives. That is exactly what we have done.

In this book, we discussed ten different areas of your life in which you can begin incorporating the LOA. Obviously, there are many more areas of your life and you can apply the LOA to anything. We want you to get the most out of the LOA as you possibly can. We feel as though the LOA has greatly shaped each of the ten outlined areas in our lives. It took time to realize what we wanted to ask the universe for, and it also took time for our dreams to manifest, but over time they did. Steve asked to live a more laid back lifestyle while accumulating wealth through his hypnotherapy practice. He asked the universe to double the sales of his online business every year. He imagined exponential growth and increased productivity every day and the universe answered Steve's request by delivering increasing growth in his business. Frank always envisioned owning a business that promoted health. He asked the universe to allow him to help others through advocating natural health. Over time, Frank was able to do this. He envisioned running his own business with employees of his own to help him promote his life's work. He also envisioned being highly profitable doing so. Today, this dream has manifested for Frank. Every day, for many days, he envisioned his dream. Now, he is living his dream.

We both wanted to incorporate things such as houses and cars into our lives. We envisioned houses with a certain number of rooms. Steve dreamed of owning additional properties that he could rent. We both envisioned our ideal car. Steve tore a picture of a Lexus SUV out of a magazine and asked the universe for it. He envisioned this specific car and was able to buy it a few years ago. All of these things have entered our lives through the use of the LOA. Frank lives in a beautiful house in New York City. Steve owns two houses in charming Savannah. Both of us drive our ideal cars. It is important to note that with time, something like a car tends to lose its "newness" and one day we will probably decide to envision a different car.

For us, the LOA is a never-ending cycle. We both feel fulfilled by what we have been able to accomplish, but we also see the great power that the LOA holds and we want to tap into this power as much as we possibly can. So we plan on asking for more and more from the universe. We have seen, felt, and realized the true power and potential of the LOA and we are in awe of it. Just as we have, we want everyone to see the true power of the LOA. You can turn your life around by incorporating these steps into your life and taking positive actions to *make things happen*. You can gain wealth. You can get a better job. You can attract your ideal mate. You can have perfect health.

Everything is right at your fingertips. Literally, this book will guide you and help you achieve your goals. The LOA is real. It worked for us; it can work for you. We want to encourage you to use the LOA, as we have, in order to attract anything and everything you want in your life.

Throughout this book we included exercises, scripts, affirmations, and other real world examples of how we incorporated the LOA into our lives. We use these exercises in our everyday lives. They have worked for us and we know they will work for you. We want to encourage you to incorporate as many of these things, as often as you can, into your every day life in order to see the biggest benefit from the LOA. We want to emphasize the importance of saturating your life with the things you want. You want to feel as if you already have what you want. You want to visualize already having it. You should visualize yourself asking for the things you want to attract and actually ask for the things you want. Your thoughts should always be positive. We cannot stress this enough.

Just as Frank pointed out in the first chapter when he told his story, surrounding yourself with positive people and incorporating positive thoughts, feelings, and actions into your life will make all the difference. We believe that Step One—Changing Negative Powers into Positive Powers—will provide you with a strong base. You cannot realistically expect to be successful with the LOA without establishing this strong base. Focus on the positive in every situation and you will feel better and be more successful with the LOA. Most important, you should thank yourself for making changes in your life. Changing your perception from negative to positive takes time and patience, but when you master this skill it will provide you with a strong and limitless base for attracting more positive things into your life.

You are in control with the LOA. No one else can control you or has power over you. You cannot attract things that you do not want deep down inside. You have to focus on things you want out of life and not what other people want. With the LOA, you must put yourself first because you are the only one who can attract things into your life—no one else can do it for you. Realize that when you take care of yourself first, you are also better able to take care of other people. For example, when you are on an airplane and the flight attendants are going over the safety guidelines before you take off, they suggest you put on your own oxygen mask before you help others around you. This is for good reason. You cannot help anyone if you yourself become incapacitated or die. You should try to apply this concept to the LOA. You must take care of yourself first. When you are able to make changes in your life and when the universe delivers great things in your life, you will then be able to help others achieve their dreams.

The power of the LOA is real. We the authors are not the only ones influenced by the LOA. Many people have incorporated the LOA into their lives and they have been able to not only greatly improve their outlook on life, but also achieve their long desired goals and dreams. Steve has been promoting the LOA to his patients for a few years now. Both of us tell our friends how we were able to get what we wanted and many of them have gone on to allowing positive things into their life with the LOA.

To this day, we are thankful for receiving the things we have received from the universe using the LOA. We are both grateful for the amazing opportunities that have come our way. We are grateful for the success we are each seeing with our respective businesses. We are thankful for the wealth we have accumulated. We are thankful for the positive personal relationships we have with friends, family, and significant others. We appreciate our health. Our work would be very difficult to do if we did not have our health. We have so much to be thankful for, more than we can possibly mention in this book. We are forever grateful to the universe for listening and answering our requests for abundance in our lives. We both feel truly abundant in all aspects of our lives. We know that you too can feel abundant in your life as well. That is why we have written this book. We wanted to spread the word on this amazing, life changing opportunity—the Law of Attraction.

References

Acitelli, L.K., Kenny, D.A., & Weiner, D. (2005). The importance of similarity and understanding of partners' marital ideals to relationship satisfaction. *Personal Relationships,* 8(2), 167–185.

Barabasz, A. & Barabasz, M. (2000). Treating AD/HD with hypnosis and neurotherapy. *Child Study Journal,* 30(1), 25–42.

Be happy. Live Longer. Optimistic Men are 50 percent less likely to die from heart disease than those less hopeful (2006, March 9). *The London Times,* p.3.

Benyamini, Y., Leventhal, E.A, & Leventhal, H. (2003). Elderly people's rating of the importance of health-related factors to their self-assessments of health. *Social Science and Medicine,* 56(8), 1661–1667.

Bray, M.A., Kehle, T.J., Peck, H.L., Margiano, S.G., Dobson, R., Peczynski, K., Gardner, K., Theodore, L.A., & Alric, J.M. (2006). Written emotional expression as an intervention for asthma: a replication. *Journal of Applied School Psychology,* 22(1), 141–165.

Caraway, K., Tucker, C.M, Reinke, W.M., & Hall, C. (2003). Self-efficacy, goal orientation, and fear of failure as predictors of school engagement in high school students. *Psychology in the Schools,* 40(4), 417–427.

Carmody, J. & Baer, R.A. (2008). Relationships between mindfulness practice and levels of mindfulness, medical and psychological symptoms and well-being in a mindfulness-based stress reduction program. *Journal of Behavioral Medicine,* 31(1), 23–33.

Centers for Disease Control and Prevention. (2009). *Heart Disease is the number one cause of death.* Retrieved from http://www.cdc.gov/Features/HeartMonth/.

Clydesdale, G. (2009). Management education's blind sport: management of workplace relations. *Journal of European Industrial Training,* 33(2), 178–191.

Delongis, A., Folkman, S. & Lazarus, R.S. (1988). The impact of daily stress on health and mood: psychological and social resources as mediators *Journal of Personality and Social Psychology,* 54(3), 486–495.

Digdon, N., Buro, K., & Sheptycki, A. (2008). Relations among mindfulness, well-being and sleep. *Personality & Individual Differences,* 45(8), 773–777. doi:10.1016/j.paid.2008.08.005

DuPont, R.L. (1997). The Selfish Brain. Washington, D.C.: American Psychiatric Press.

Emoto, M. (2004). *The hidden messages in water.* Beyond Words Publishing.

Erber, R. & Erber, M.W. (2000). The self-regulation of moods: Second thoughts on the importance of happiness in everyday life. *Psychological Inquiry,* 11(3), 142–148.

Hill, N. (1987) *Think and Grow Rich.* Ballantine Books.

Holder, M. & Coleman, B. (2009). The contribution of social relationships to children's happiness. *Journal of Happiness Studies,* 10(3), 329–3494.

Jackson, E.S., Tucker, C.M., & Herman, K.C. (2007). Health value, perceived social support, and health self-efficacy as factors in a health-promoting lifestyle. *Journal of American College Health,* 56(1), 69–74.

Jones, S.G. (2007). Inductions and Deepenings Volume I.

Jones, S.G. (2007). Basic Hypnotherapy for Professionals.

Karasek, R.A. (2004). An analysis of 19 international case studies of stress prevention through work reorganization using the demand/control model. *Bulletin of Science Technology and Society,* 24(5), 446–456.

Kotz, D. Get happy and you'll live longer. (2006, December 26). *US News & World Report.*

Kruger, J. & Kohll, H.W. (2008). Prevalence of regular physical activity among adults—United States, 2001 and 20005. *Journal of the American Medical Association,* 299(1), 30–32.

Lyubomirsky, S., King, L., & Diener, E. (2005). The benefits of frequent positive affect: does happiness lead to success? *Psychological Bulletin,* 131(6), 803–855.

McGowan, K. (2005). Learning to love the lotus. *Psychology Today,* 38(5), 30–32.

Miller, J.R. (1994). Fear of success: psychodynamic implications. *Journal of American Academy of Psychoanalysis,* 22, 129–136.

Muris, P., Mayer, B., den Adel, M., Roos, T., & van Wamelen, J. (2009). Predictors of change following cognitive-behavioral treatment of children with anxiety problems: a preliminary investigation on negative automatic thoughts and anxiety control. *Child Psychiatry and Human Development,* 40(1), 139–151.

Paivandy, S., Bullock, E.E., Reardon, R.C., & Kelly, F.D. (2008). The effects of decision—making style and cognitive thought patterns on negative career thoughts. *Journal of Career Assessment,* 16(4), 474–488.

Petocz, P. & Sowey, E. (2008). Statistical diversions. *Teaching Statistics: An International Journal for Teachers,* 30(3), 93–96.

Prisbell, M. & Andersen, J.F. (1980). The importance of perceived homophily, level of uncertainty, feeling good, safety, and self-disclosure in interpersonal relationships. *Communication Quarterly,* 28(3), 22–33.

Ritz, P. & Berrut, G. (2008). The importance of good hydration for day-to-day health. *Nutrition News,* 63(1), S6-S13.

Robson, S.M.& Hansson, R.O. (2007). Strategic self development for successful aging at work. *International Journal of Aging and Human Development,* 64(4), 331–359.

Russell, R.J.H. & Wells, P.A. (1994). Predictors of happiness in married couples. *Personality and Individual Differences,* 17(3), 313–321.

Smith, J.T. (1996). Comparison of hypnosis and distraction in severely ill children undergoing painful medical procedures. *Journal of Counseling Psychology,* 43(2), 187–195.

Taylor, S.E., Peplau, L.A. & Sears, D.O. (2000). *Social Psychology* (10th ed). Upper Saddle River, NJ: Prentice Hall.

Tucker, K. (2007) Getting the most out of life: an examination of appreciation, targets of appreciation, and sensitivity to reward in happier and less happy individuals. *Journal of Social & Clinical Psychology,* 26(7), 791–825.

Van Ecke, Y. (2007). Attachment style and dysfunctional career thoughts: How attachment style can affect the career counseling process. *Career Development Quarterly,* 55(4), 339–350.

Veenhoven et al. (2008). Healthy happiness: effects of happiness on physical health and the consequences for preventative health care. *Journal of Happiness Studies,* 9(3), 449—456. doi:10.1007/ 10902–006–9042–1.

Wattles, W.D. (2008) *The Science of Getting Rich.* BN Publishing.

Index

cigarette 123
clothes 115
clothing 33
Clydesdale (2009) 89
cognitive function 125
complaint-free holiday 201
computers 115
concentration 147
condominium 112
confidence 67
conflict 8
contentment 28
control 55
cortisol 70
country club membership 115
courage 19
creative visualization 34
creator 51
crystals 15

D
decisions 98
deepening 170
defeat 160
Deirdre Dyson 52
Delongis, 1988 76
delta 169
demons 18
depressed 8
desires 20
detachment 188
diabetes 77
Digdon, Buro & Sheptycki, 2008
    125
disappointment 28
disease 76
disempowerment 28
doctors 17
Dr. Masaru Emoto 15
dreams viii
drugs 124
DuPont, 1997 85

E
eating right 117

e-book 6
educated 38
EFT 199
ego 2
Eileen Caddy 65
electromagnetic waves 14
electronics 115
emotional 1, 9
Emotional Freedom Technique 199
emotions 21
empowerment 28
endorphins 120
energy 14
engine 118
enjoying 163
enthusiasm 28
entrepreneurial spirit 7
Erber & Erber, 2000 69
exercise 70

F
fate 53
fear of failure 36
fear of success 36
feelings vii, 10
finances 95
financial 1
financial health 11
financial independence 8
food 124
fortune 97
frequency 14
friendship 50
fulfillment 6
furniture 115

G
gambling 124
goals viii, 3
gratitude 16
gratitude journal 41
gratitude list 41
growth 125

About Steve G. Jones

Steve G. Jones is a board certified Clinical Hypnotherapist. He has been practicing hypnotherapy since the 1980s. He is the author of twenty-two books on hypnotherapy. Jones has over twenty years experience as a certified clinical hypnotherapist, both teaching hypnotherapy students and working with clients. His list of former clients include: Danny Bonaduce, Jeraldine Saunders (creator of the "Love Boat" TV series), Tom Mankiewicz (writer of the "Superman" movie), and many other celebrities. He has served on the board of directors of the American Lung Association in Los Angeles, California. He is a member of the National Guild of Hypnotists, National Board of Certified Clinical Hypnotherapists, founder of the American Alliance of Hypnotists, member of the International Registry of Clinical Hypnotherapists, has presented his hypnotherapy research at the American Council of Hypnotists Examiners, received the President's appreciation award for his outstanding contributions to the American Association for Adult and Continuing Education, is a member of the American Board of Hypnotherapy, member of Who's Who among Students in American Universities and Colleges, member of Pi Lambda Theta International Honor Society and Professional Association in Education, member of Omicron Delta Kappa Honor Society, member of the Golden Key Honor Society, and recipient of the National Leadership Award from the United States National Congressional Committee.

In the mid 1980s, Jones began study at the University of Florida. His primary research focus was cognitive psychology, understanding how people learn. Much of his early research was published in psychology journals in late 1980s. Meanwhile, he continued practicing hypnosis outside of academia on a regular basis.

From 1990 to 1995, he was fortunate to counsel families and individuals. During this time he finished his degree in psychology at the University of Florida and went on to graduate studies in counseling. He has a bachelor's degree in psychology from the University of Florida (1994), a master's degree in education from Armstrong Atlantic State University (2007), received his educational specialist degree from Georgia Southern University, and is currently working on a doctorate in education, Ed.D., at Georgia Southern University.

Jones sees clients for a variety of conditions. Among them are: weight loss, anxiety, smoking cessation, test taking, phobias (such as fear of flying), nail biting, road rage, anger management, IBS, general wellness, pre-surgical and pre-dental pain control, natural childbirth, and many others.

In business settings, he is regularly called upon by sales teams to boost salesperson motivation. His straightforward techniques have significantly and consistently increased sales.

Jones also works extensively with Hollywood actors, writers, directors, and producers, helping them achieve their very best. He has recently been featured on TruTV, CNN, and is under a development contract for his new television series on hypnotherapy. Learn more at: http://www.BetterLivingWithHypnosis.com.

About Frank Mangano

Frank Mangano is an American author, researcher, health advocate and entrepreneur in the field of alternative health. He was born August 9th, 1977 in New York City where he still currently resides. Mangano is the author of several books including *The 60 Day Prescription Free Cholesterol Cure*, *The Mind Killer Defense*, which he co-authored with Dr. Cynthia Foster, M.D. and Kim Wierman, *You Can Attract It*, which he co-authored with Clinical Hypnotherapist Steve G. Jones and *The Blood Pressure Miracle*, which hit best seller in three categories on Amazon.com within days of its release. Additionally, he has published numerous reports and a considerable amount of articles pertaining to natural health.

When asked how his interest in alternative medicine first began, he once responded by saying, "Since as far back as I can remember, prescription drugs always scared me. I always felt that if nature created a problem; it also had a solution." He started vitamin/mineral supplementation in his early teen years and now has a vast knowledge of how supplementation can be used to treat and prevent illnesses, diseases, ailments, infections, viruses and other health conditions. His insight is present in hundreds of articles related to this topic.

Mangano's strong passion for helping others improve their health inexpensively and naturally transformed into his full-time career and life mission when his mother was diagnosed with high cholesterol in the early 2000's. Her fear of the side effects associated with taking prescription drugs like statins led her to turn to him for help.

Determined to find a method for her to lower her cholesterol naturally, Mangano studied and reviewed medical books, reports, articles and case studies as well as literature on natural herbs, vitamins and minerals. After months of research, he synergistically combined all of his acquired knowledge and created a plan based on science that allowed her to lower her cholesterol without drugs. Her cholesterol dropped nearly forty points with his all-natural system. Wanting to help more people, he wrote and self-published his first book called, *The 60 Day Prescription-Free Cholesterol Cure*. The book is now helping numerous people worldwide lower their cholesterol naturally.

Mangano focuses a big portion of his time building and managing Natural Health on the Web, which offers readers free and valuable information on alternative remedies. The site contains information on an extensive amount of conditions, which can be treated and prevented using natural methods. Learn more at:

http://www.NaturalHealthOnTheWeb.com

Breinigsville, PA USA
22 July 2010
242292BV00001B/204/P